LIFE SENTENCES

HOW YOU CHANGE LIVES WITH WORDS

Larry W. Dennis, Sr.

Other books by Larry W. Dennis, Sr.

15 Principles of Engaging Leadership

The Language of Leadership:
Communicating for Results

Repeat Business:
6 Steps to Superior Customer Service

How to Turbocharge You:
6 Steps to Tap Your True Potential

Information in Formation:
How to Gain the 71% Advantage

Making Moments Matter:
89 Tools for Taking Charge of Your Time

15 Leadership Principles & Ronald Reagan:
Use Them to Change Your World

Motorcycle Meditations:
A Vision Quest to Alaska

The Great Baseball Cap
(a children's book)

Life Sentences
First Printing 2018

For information, contact the publisher:
Rising Tide Publishing
admin@turbols.com

ISBN: 978-0-9631766-5-3
Library of Congress Control Number: 2018952892

Cover design: Richard Ferguson

Manufactured in the U.S.A.

Table of Contents

PREFACE

"The golden moments in the stream of life rush past us
and we see nothing but sand;
the angels come to visit us,
and we only know them when they are gone."
George Elliot

LIFE SENTENCES is for purposeful people who desire to make a meaningful difference in the lives of others. By following the inspiration and direction in LIFE SENTENCES, you will enhance the quality, purpose, and impact of your life. Most important of all, you will experience significance as you exercise your authority to grant *life sentences* to those you love, lead, live, and work with.

"Our speech, a powerful means, reveals our ends.
Our speech attracts or repels, praises or condemns,
inspires or disheartens, honors or dishonors,
conciliates or antagonizes, enlightens or deludes,
identifies or obscures, unifies or divides –
and thus with each, expressed thought advances good or evil."
William W. Bayes

William Bayes is right. Every word you utter has the potential to make a lifelong impact on others. Your sentences have more power, and your words have more impact than you know or imagine. In fact, your judgment can free or imprison others for a lifetime.

INTRODUCTION

"Optimism is essential to achievement
and it is also the foundation of courage and of true progress."
Nicholas Murray Butler

There I was, sitting in Eastern Michigan University's auditorium, anxiously listening to the freshman orientation. I felt out of place and unsure of myself as I heard "What every freshman should know." Toward the end of the program, "Bingo" Brown the Dean of Men stiffly walked out on the stage. He leaned on the back of a chair placed there to support him. In his strong, booming, authoritative voice, he said, "Welcome to Eastern Michigan University." I sat straight up, mesmerized by his presence. I was amazed at the power of this soon-to-be retiring legendary professor and coach. Later in the week, I was required to meet with the dean one-on-one. I nervously walked into his office. He offered a chair and asked me a few questions. We talked about my plans, why I had enrolled, and what I hoped to gain for my career and future. He told me what would be required for me to succeed. As I got up to leave, Dr. Brown looked at me and said in his authoritative tone, "Dennis, with a smile like yours, you'll be successful in whatever you do." I walked out of his office reassured with my head in the air. I felt ten feet tall.

I had been, to put it mildly, a poor student in high school, graduating from Ypsilanti High School near the bottom of my class. My first term at Eastern Michigan University, I made the Dean's List. What a shift! One sentence, "with a smile like yours," from this powerful person was, for me, a *life sentence.*

Praise, put downs, criticism, or supportive, encouraging words from a person you respect, someone of authority you look up to, can permanently change the direction of your life, can be a *life sentence*!

The term "sentence" comes from the Latin word "*sententia*," which originally meant "opinion," "decision," or "judgment." A "sentence" was the length of time that a person would be restrained.

A legal life sentence is a declaration issued by an authority, a judge who has been vested by the state with the power to restrain the individual who is arraigned before them.

When you think of a life sentence, what picture comes to mind? Being sent to prison for life with no hope of parole? There are approximately 65,000 judges in America who are given the authority and power to declare a life sentence. Their decree can force you to live behind bars in a prison cell for the rest of your life. As you read and ponder the ideas in LIFE SENTENCES you will see how your sentences can free or imprison those you have influence with for a lifetime.

"You don't learn to walk by following rules.
You learn by doing and falling over."
Richard Branson

Escape Artist

The famous escape artist, Harry Houdini, could open any lock, escape from any restraint – ropes, trunks, chains, strait jackets, even under water. In 1900, he was placed inside a bank vault in England with the condition that he unlock the vault door in four minutes.

Houdini's contracts always specified that before he disappeared into the trunk, cell, or behind a small curtain (when performing on a stage), he could kiss his wife. After all, many of his feats were seriously dangerous, so who could refuse the couple what might be their last goodbye? No one knew he was getting more than a kiss! As their lips met, his wife would secretly pass a small piece of wire from her mouth to his. Then, once he was alone, he'd use the wire to pick the locks. This time, the wire didn't do the trick. Here's what Houdini wrote about that experience:

"After one solid minute, I didn't hear any of the familiar clicking sounds. I thought, my gosh, this could ruin my career. I'm at the pinnacle of fame and the press is all here.

"After two minutes, the pressure was on. I was beginning to sweat profusely because I was not getting the lock picked.

"After three minutes of failure, with thirty seconds left, I nervously reached into my pocket for a handkerchief to dry my hands and forehead, and when I did, I inadvertently leaned against the vault door and it creaked open."

No wonder he couldn't unlock it - it was never locked! All he had to do was push and the door swung open.

There you have it, my friend. The door was never locked! Harry had been told it was locked. He believed the door was locked and it might as well have been locked. Only the accident of leaning on the door changed that belief and saved his career.

To create breakthroughs in your life, carefully examine what you believe is "possible" and "impossible" for you. Investigate the doors of opportunity you feel are locking you out. Who said you couldn't or shouldn't? When did you decide you shouldn't do that, wouldn't be that, couldn't own that?

"You will never be free until you free yourself from the prison of your own false thoughts."
Philip Arnold

Here Comes the Judge

More than likely, you've never experienced the terror of being locked in a vault or the trauma of standing before a robed judge, waiting to hear the verdict. You have seen enough movies, television reenactments, and newscasts to know the power of the robed judge. You've heard judges proclaim, "By the power vested in me, I sentence you to life in prison without parole." You witnessed the devastation and tears, or relief and shouts of joy that often come with that final sentence. Think of the power of such a pronouncement to liberate or imprison a person for the rest of their life.

Very few people will ever stand before a robed judge and receive a life sentence. All of us have experienced the impact of the judgments of authority figures in your life. You have heard sentences which have affected the rest of your life. Even though there are only 65,000 judges given the authority to decree a literal life in jail sentence, you have been on the receiving end of countless *life sentences* from the influential people in your life.

"No love, no friendship can cross the path of our destiny without leaving some mark on it forever."
Francois Muriac

You and I live in a cell known as our self-image formed before we were seven-years-old by decrees, the *life sentences* of authority figures in our lives. You have this same power, the authority to issue *life sentences.* It's as if they stand before you awaiting your judgment, your *life sentence.* Your declaration can determine their future, their destiny. You can unlock doors for them.

LIFE SENTENCES shows you how to . . .

- Declare liberating *life sentences*
- Unlock the doors you struggle to open
- Discover positive *life sentences* you have forgotten
- Eliminate falsely imposed limitations
- Break out of your limiting cells
- Gain purpose in setting others free
- Live a liberated life, free from false beliefs that limit you

The Premises

Our lives, who we are, how we think of ourselves is a construct of our memories. We can choose which memories to rehearse, nurse, review, revitalize, and imbue with feeling. Negative memories can seem to be and perhaps by nature are more powerful. But you can change this. You can take charge of your memories.

How? You can only hold one thought at a time. Thoughts may and do often dart through our minds at a high rate of speed. Still we are thinking one thought at a time. You can change your future by taking charge of your thoughts and feelings about the experiences you remember. And so when you recall negative memories, pictures that call up limiting feelings about yourself – don't try to stop these old tapes.

Instead, replace them with a new thought, an uplifting picture, and the feelings that accompany your positive memory.

Our three primary premises could at first seem contradictory.

The first premise: Declarations by influential people have determined the quality, nature, and trajectory of your life.

The second premise: You are far more influential in the lives of others than you have ever imagined. Your declarations will limit and restrain the liberty of others or you can grant them life, power, and purpose for the rest of their lives.

And our third premise: You can lean against any falsely limiting door, be granted a pardon, and escape from the erroneous prisons of your past. You no longer need to be the prisoner of destructive *life sentences.*

"Fix your eyes forward for what you can do, not back on what you cannot change."
Tom Clancey

Discernment

To live an empowered life, a full life, a life of purpose, joy, meaning, and true significance, you must learn to discern the real truth about yourself. When we were children, the declarations influential adults made about us were defining – cute or homely, fit or chubby, smart or dumb, clumsy or graceful, slow or quick, bashful or friendly. These declarations were accepted as gospel. As adults, we must set aside, put behind us childish things. Now we must discern for ourselves the whole truth, the real truth about ourselves. Few of us ever rise above being defined by the declaration of authority figures whose opinions we respected or whose approval and love we desired.

Most analysis examines negative childhood experiences, relationships, and other important influences of authority figures. This analysis is applied to dysfunctional adults who are struggling to make their lives work. Even those of us who might be defined as fully functional are barely scratching the surface of our potential. We begin our journey of self-discovery by setting aside the limiting stories we have accepted about ourselves and believe more of the truth about our greatness.

Many years ago, I read a powerful little book by J. Martin

Kohe, titled *Your Greatest Power.* What is your greatest power? Your greatest power is the power to choose your thoughts. You have a choice. You can choose to think of the powerful, positive *life sentences* you were given, or take the easy path and think of negative, diminishing *life sentences.* We seem to easily remember the negative, limiting things others said about us. We naturally put an emotional charge on negative declarations. By learning to recall and amplify positive declarations with an electric, emotional charge, you leverage for greater effect every empowering declaration made about you.

"The art of living lies less in eliminating our troubles than growing with them."
Bernard M. Baruch

Yes You Can

The purpose of this book is to help you reach more of your full potential while helping others reach more of their potential. We will devote no time to asking you to remember, relive, and analyze limiting or destructive declarations others made about you. We are challenging you, through a process of self-discovery, to re-member, to be re-minded, to re-connect with the positive declarations, positive *life sentences* others made about you. Their *life sentences* empowered you to enjoy your many successes to become who and be where you are today. We believe that someone, and probably many someone's along your way, commented on your talent, capabilities, skills, unique characteristics, and positive qualities. These thoughtful comments of respected people contributed to your awareness of and amplified your strengths. You are today who you are in large measure because of those declarations. Getting in touch with remembering these positive declarations is freeing and empowering. This exercise can literally reenergize you, turbocharge you as you begin a whole new chapter in your life. Some of the declarations you'll remember were more powerful because they came at a time when you were fearful, experiencing setbacks, or attempting a doubtful task. Then someone of influence issued a *life sentence*, declared a positive outcome, told you that you could accomplish, do, be, have, the thing that seemed so out of reach, so impossible to achieve. And you courageously took the next step.

"The heart, like the mind, has a memory.
And in it are kept the most precious keepsakes."
Henry Wadsworth Longfellow

Life Purpose

You reach your highest life purpose when you make positive declarations, *life sentences* that help others see their potential, their strengths, and believe in their possibilities. These are the positive *life sentences* you alone can declare.

Since I have the advantage of thinking about these ideas for decades, I have several personal examples to share. I share my examples, along with examples of friends, clients, and class members, as a way to stimulate you to think about the people in your life who provided the encouragement, stimulation, insightful declarations that were positive *life sentences* for you.

"Throughout all history, the great wise men and teachers,
philosophers, and prophets have disagreed
with one another on many different things.
It is only on this one point that they are in complete and unanimous
agreement – we become what we think about."
- Earl Nightingale

Remembering and writing out my positive *life sentences* has helped me realize how fortunate I have been—not that I didn't experience my share of negative declarations. I am sure I must have. Over 40 years ago, I began to inventory in writing and reflect on my positive *life sentences.* Any negative, destructive things said about me have long ago faded from memory.

LIFE SENTENCES draws on real-life experiences of front-line supervisors, department heads, and executive team members. Nothing could be more credible than their real-world stories demonstrating how they put these ideas to the test in the daily challenges of leadership.

Some "Turbo terms" you will find in the following chapters include:

The "Person Pearl"™ Managers apply the 15 Leadership Principles with their chosen "Person Pearl." The thread of the "Person Pearl" runs through many of the true-life stories you will read.

5X More Enthusiasm™ Leadership Development Lab members report amazing results when they focus five times (5X) more concentrated energy on important projects.

The 15 Leadership Principles™ form the foundational framework for everything we have done in Turbo Leadership Systems leadership training programs over the past 30 years. The stories of how leaders have used these 15 principles to increase their effectiveness are throughout LIFE SENTENCES.

1. Lead from high ideals
2. Become genuinely interested
3. Don't criticize, condemn or complain
4. Provide acknowledgement
5. See the other person's point of view
6. Be an active listener
7. Play yourself down
8. Validate the other person's ideas
9. Dramatize your ideas
10. Stimulate competition
11. When you blow it, show it
12. Avoid dogmatic declarations
13. Avoid arguments
14. Begin with yes, yes, yes
15. Appeal to the other person's noble motives

Chapter One

"How far that light the candle throws its beams!
So shines a good deed in a naughty world."
William Shakespeare

GOOD JUDGMENT

Dr. Robert Schuller, founder of the Crystal Cathedral in Garden Grove, California, loved to tell the story of his missionary uncle returning from China to the family farm in Iowa. Bob was only five-years-old. His uncle scooped him up in his arms, threw him in the air and said, "So, you're Robert. You're going to be a great minister someday." And so he was. Starting from scratch with no building, conducting Sunday services in a drive-in theater, he grew his church, Crystal Cathedral Ministries, to a three thousand-seat sanctuary and an international television audience of more than a million world-wide viewers.

"Accept no one's definition of your life; define yourself."
Harvey Fierstein

Young at Heart

When we were young and impressionable, we believed everything people said about us. We accepted the pronouncements of significant people as gospel—as the "whole truth and nothing but the truth." As we grow in experience, we edit the pronouncements of others through the filters we develop. When we are "new" at anything - working at a new job, a new athletic endeavor, or a new relationship - we are vulnerable and extremely impressionable. We may only filter a few of the comments made about us.

"Everything I am or ever hope to be, I owe to my angel mother."
Abraham Lincoln

Cover Girl

Lisa, the office manager for an equipment rental company told us: "I was in the third grade. It was time for the annual Camp Fire Girls Candy Sale. My mother, who was also my Camp Fire troop leader, said, 'Lisa, you can sell 84 boxes of candy and win the contest.' There was a certainty in her voice that inspired and convinced me I could.

"The first day of the sale my mother picked me up at school, and I started selling feverishly at 4:00. After knocking on every door in my neighborhood, it was off to store fronts, apartment complexes, family and friends, selling boxes of candy. Luckily for me, the candy sale only lasted 14 days. My mom, who was serving as my chauffeur, cheerleader, and enthusiastic coach, maintained her confidence and belief that no one could resist my sales pitch and cute smile.

"Every day for those two weeks, I persistently knocked on doors. My hard work and dedication did pay off. I was one of the Portland area's highest-volume candy sellers that year. My reward was being chosen as the cover girl for the following year, with my picture on the front of the 1975 Camp Fire candy brochure.

"The lesson I learned from this experience is how powerful a mother's declared belief can be. My mother's belief in me gave me belief in myself. Her support and encouragement set in motion a pattern of persistence that lasts to this day."

I wish we had more moms like Lisa's! Moms who believe deeply in their children, who make declarative statements ("you can sell 84 boxes of candy"), and go to work coaching them to greatness. We need more moms who recognize that nagging, critical comments can hold their children back and keep them stuck. We need more moms who bless their children with positive statements of belief which can and do propel them to persistence in the pursuit of goals.

"The foolish man seeks happiness in the distance; the wise grows it under his feet."
Lamar Oppenheimer

Engineer's Road to Success

Dave, the yard fabrication manager for Hamilton Construction, told us: "In the summer of 1959, I was nine-years-old. We lived in Empire, Oregon, a small community on the outskirts of Coos Bay. I was just hanging around the house with nothing much to do.

"The street in front of our house was gravel; the city had contracted to pave all the streets in my area of town. I was fascinated as I watched the graders, dump trucks, and cement trucks come and go in front of our house. Then one day, I decided this is the kind of work I would like to do someday. I started hanging around the guys who were doing the work. When it came time for breaks, I would run to the store to buy them a pop or whatever snack they wanted, and then again, at lunchtime I would buy them stuff they wanted from our neighborhood store.

"Soon I was one of the regular "guys" going around to all of their work sites with them. I pulled nails out of the used framing boards, helped load up lumber and pretty much did anything I could to help the guys. Hard to believe, they let me help. I know today the laws wouldn't let a nine-year old help like I did.

"My routine continued all summer. It was great being able to help the crew and feel good about what I was doing. By late August, they finished the last job in our part of town. When the guys packed up and headed home, they all thanked me for my part and seemed to really appreciate what I had done to help out.

"That fall, on September 10, after school had started, I got a letter from Fred C. Dyer, the city manager of Empire, thanking me for the work I had done. They bestowed on me the title of "Honorary Assistant Engineer" for the city of Empire, Coos County, Oregon. Pretty big stuff for a nine-year old.

"Today I am a registered engineer. I've worked for over 25 years with Hamilton Construction, a bridge-building firm I am very proud of. We build bridges throughout the Western states. Last year we received the #1 Contractor Award by the Oregon Department of Transportation (ODOT). Fred Dyer gave me a lasting *life sentence* over 40 years ago."

As you travel through life and come to forks in the road or those inevitable puddles, creeks, and raging rivers *life sentences* build the bridges for you to cross to your secure future. A future where you can be seen as number one.

"Why are you trying so hard to fit in
when you were born to stand out."
Oliver James

Summer Camp

Mrs. Dixon, my fourth grade teacher, nominated me to attend the University of Michigan's Fresh Air Camp. This was a camp for disadvantaged boys from troubled homes. Somehow, she arranged for me to secure a scholarship. It was an experience I'll never forget. I had the rare opportunity that summer to play unrestrained, finally learning how to swim and just be a carefree kid.

Toward the end of the two-week camp, we had a carnival with games and prizes. Every camper was given 24 tickets to spend on the things they wanted to do in the various booths. Our cabin counselor challenged us to create an arcade game that would collect more tickets than any other attraction. The highlight of my previous summers was spending every nickel I could scrape together to buy tickets for rides and games at the Fourth of July carnival. I took charge. I told the guys in my cabin what we should do and how to holler "Right this way! Step right up!" In our game, the contestant threw a baseball 15 feet to knock down a pyramid of six stacked milk bottles we had weighted down with sand. If they knocked down all six they won a prize. We took in more tickets than any other cabin's game and won first place. Our reward was candy, fresh fruit, and most important, the recognition for having the #1 attraction. I received compliments from the counselors on my leadership and our booth's success. Their comments about my leadership and creativity were *life sentences* that made me feel like a winner.

Your life works better when you filter the negative things said about you. Make a game of finding and remembering the positive declarations others made about you. Build a pyramid of positive statements and stabilize them like we did by adding sand to our milk bottles. Do this and you will WIN.

"The greatest and most important problems of life
are all fundamentally insoluble.
They can never be solved but only outgrown."
Carl Jung

Safety Patrol

As I think about the *life sentences* I've been given, I can't help wondering if my sixth grade teacher Mr. Fletcher, a wounded World War II veteran, realized what a *life sentence* he was giving me when he appointed me lieutenant on the Woodruff Grade School Safety Patrol. There were no adults at corner crosswalks in those days. Our school was on Michigan Avenue, which was the busiest street in our town. Mr. Fletcher said, "Larry, I am appointing you captain because you have natural leadership abilities."

It's hard to express how important it was for me to be given this reputation, and how different the reputation was from my own self-appraisal. It must have made a meaningful impression if I remember the incident as clearly as I do fifty years later.

What about you? Can you think of some *life sentences* given to you at an early age by a community leader, teacher, or a parent?

I wonder if my mother knew the *life sentence* she was giving me when, at the age of 11, she gave me the authority to go uptown after school to Smith's Furniture and pick out a chrome-legged, Formica-topped dinette table-and-chairs set they had on sale. A few days later, when the table and chairs arrived, what a *life sentence* she gave me by telling me what a good decision I had made about the color and style I had chosen.

"There is a great man who makes every man feel small.
But the real great man is the man
who makes every man feel great."
G. K. Chesterton

Peddling Papers

When I was twelve, I took over my neighborhood Detroit News paper route. The only problem was I didn't own a decent bicycle. My mother and I went down to Congdon's Hardware on Pearl Street. Mr. Congdon granted me a *life sentence* when, at age 12, I signed the paperwork to buy my new blue Columbia bicycle on a weekly payment plan. Mr. Congdon told my mother, "This is between Larry and I." He shook my hand and said, "I'll trust you to make the $2.00-a-week payments." I made the payments each week. What a boost to my self-confidence. About six months later, as I was making my last payments, I finally gathered the courage to ask Mr. Congdon if he would hire me as a delivery boy when I turned 16. He said, "Yes."

"Thinking will not overcome fear but action will."
W. Clement Stone

Four Point

Mike, foreman for Cascade Acoustics, told us: "Ever since my wife and I married ten years ago and began having a family, our children have been the focus of our life. We made it a priority to spend a lot of one-on-one time with them reading, teaching, and playing. We coached baseball, basketball, and wrestling for their teams. We have been Cub Scout and Girl Scout leaders and always worked at being parents and friends.

"Last May, our twelve-year-old daughter's teacher sent home a letter telling us that Jessica had been selected for the Presidential Education Award because of her 3.8 grade average throughout her six years of grade school. As you can imagine, we were very proud of her, and of course went to the awards presentation. When she received her award, my wife cried. I tried not to because it's hard to videotape through tears.

"When I saw how proud Jessica was of her award, I decided to e-mail President Clinton and thank him for his help in keeping our children motivated. I wrote, 'This award focuses on academic achievement and is a big help with all the distractions and extracurricular activities our kids are facing today.'

"About a month after sending the e-mail, to our amazement, we received an original copy of the letter of congratulations addressed to our daughter, complete with the Presidential seal and an original Presidential signature. Our daughter was even more excited now with the personal letter addressed to her from the President of the United States.

"Recently, we received her first middle school report card, and she has a 4.0 grade average. Nothing has been so powerful for our daughter as the *life sentence* she received from the President of the United States."

"Success is not final, failure is not fatal;
it is the courage to continue that counts."
Winston Churchill

Headmaster

Arlette, customer service supervisor for a Bay Area international telecommunications company, told us: "My family is originally from France. I was born and raised in Africa until the age of fourteen. In my eighth grade year we moved to France. It was a hard transition for me. Life in France was very different from life in Africa.

"At the end of the eighth grade, my teachers decided that I should repeat the year. My father thought they were making a mistake. He made an appointment with the headmaster. I was asked to be there too. At the time of the meeting, they made me kneel in a corner, facing the wall. The headmaster explained to my father that, 'all of the teachers had come to the same conclusion—I was a very nice girl, not very bright, but pretty. The headmaster told my father, 'Don't worry. She will find a good husband and in the meantime, she should go to a trade school.'

"My father refused to give up. He continued to argue on my behalf. After a very long meeting, I was trembling in the corner from the humiliation. By the time we walked out of the school that morning, my father had convinced the headmaster that I be allowed to go on to the ninth grade.

"I passed the ninth grade! In the eleventh and twelfth grades, I was very lucky to have two exceptional teachers who believed in me and showed it. Because of their *life sentences,* I began to regain my self-confidence and once again believed in myself.

"After graduating from high school, I attended one of the top universities in France, where I majored in Political Science and Administrative Law. I graduated from the university with honors. I went on to earn a BA in psychology from the John F. Kennedy University in Orinda, California, where I made the Dean's List.

"The lesson I learned from my experience is another person's opinion of me is only their perception. I don't have to accept their judgment. The headmaster's perception of me as not being very bright didn't mean I wasn't. It took me many years to realize how much her critical, demeaning *life sentence* affected me. I know now that I didn't have to accept their declaration as true."

Arlett's story shows us clearly that we can choose to remember the negative or the positive things people say about us. Ultimately, it is up to us to take charge of our memories. Remember the wonderful teachers and forget the negative headmasters in your life.

"The only way on earth to multiply happiness is to divide it."
Paul Scherer

Hey Coach

It was the fall of 1956. I was a junior at Ypsilanti High School. Back to school is an exciting time. Everyone was reconnecting, figuring out what classes we were in, and who our teachers were. Between bells, the halls of my old school were crowded shoulder-to-shoulder with kids, hustling to make it to the next class. I felt a tap on my shoulder and turned around. It was Mr. Dewsbeaver, who had been my history teacher the year before. He said, "Dennis, are you going out for football?"

Being on the football team was a very big deal in my school. I said, "I don't think so."

He said, "Well, I can get you on the team."

I said, "Thanks," and kept on moving. I hadn't played football in junior high. I had never gone out for sports; I always worked after school. I can still hear the lockers slamming in the hall as I think about this experience. I never thought of myself as having athletic ability. That tap on the shoulder helped me see myself differently. I felt more capable because Mr. Dewsbeaver's *life sentence*, as brief as it was, strengthened my self-esteem. In some important ways, my history teacher, Mr. Dewsbeaver, gave me a *life sentence* that changed my history.

"Dignity does not consist in possessing honors,
but in the consciousness that we deserve them."
Aristotle

Picture Perfect

When I was nearing graduation, my mother took my black and white senior picture proofs to our minister, Rev. Jonathan Winters, to ask for his advice about which one we should choose. He said, "That's the one Larry ought to pick. It will look good on his desk someday." At that time in my life, I couldn't dimly imagine myself ever working in an office or having a desk. His comment implied being a business executive, which was a hundred miles from the picture I held in my head of my future. My minister helped me see myself differently; he gave me a *life sentence*, a different picture of my future.

"Only one thing has to change
for us to know happiness in our lives;
where we focus our attention."
Greg Anderson

Playing Catch

In April of 1958, I went to see my Uncle Jerry O'Neil down in Chillicothe, Ohio. I left right after work and got there late Saturday night. The next morning, he and I went to the jobsite. He was superintendent on an interstate right of way bridge construction project in the area. Later in the day, we were playing catch beside his mobile home, talking about my future. It was only a matter of a few weeks now before I would be graduating from high school. My plan had always been to go to work for Uncle Jerry. I thought he had promised me a job. It was easy for me to picture myself working on construction projects, "following in my family's footsteps." Maybe someday I could be superintendent. Uncle Jerry made fantastic money. I had heard he made over $12,000 a year! That was a fortune as far as I was concerned.

As we pitched the football back and forth, he said something that was double-edged and changed the course of my life. The first thing he said was, "Larry, I'm not going to hire you when you graduate from high school." I was in shock. I could barely catch the ball. I didn't know what to say. He went on, "I think there's something better for you." It was hard for me to imagine anything better. Still, there was something about the way he said "better for you" that made me believe he meant it. I was relieved when he went on to say, "If you're not able to find something else, come back, and see me."

I tried to hang on to "I think there's something better for you." That statement affirmed me, gave me the thrust, self-confidence, and motivation to set into motion a completely new plan of what I would do when I graduated. His affirmation helped me believe that I wouldn't fumble, that I would hold on to the ball. His *life sentence* dramatically changed the direction of my life.

"God gave us memory so that we might have roses in December."
James M. Barrie

Slip Sliding Away

Jim, director of produce for a food distribution company, told us: "It was spring of 1956, I was twenty-three-years-old and had just finished my company's eleven-week sales training program. I was so eager to be in sales that by working a double shift I actually finished the training in six weeks. I was scheduled to relieve a regular sales associate during his two-week vacation. This was my first day. It was necessary for my first call to be very early in the morning to allow time to finish all the other calls that day.

"I lived in Portland. It took an hour-and-a-half to drive to Cougar in those days. I got up at 4:00 A.M. It wasn't hard because I was too excited to sleep anyway.

"Donned in my best and only hand-me-down double-breasted suit and my leather-soled 'English brogue' shoes, I headed out the door for my first call as a salesman. I pulled into the prison camp parking area just after daybreak. I could see the prison mess hall. The wide covered porch was packed with big "toughs" smoking and drinking coffee. One of the big guys wore a white cook uniform and a big apron. That was Bo, the head cook. I was supposed to see him to write up their order. There were no gutters on the building and water was pouring off the porch roof. The dim morning light made these guys look bigger and meaner. I was not just intimidated I was scared to death. I wanted to turn around drive off, but I was a salesman on my first call and this was it!

"Invoice book and catalog in hand, I got out of the car.

Mud and water were standing on both sides of the three feet wide board walkway leading to the building. Throwing my shoulders back, I courageously started up the walkway. About half way in, forgetting I had metal taps on the heels of my brogues, I slipped! Down I went in the muck, my left foot up to my knee and my arm nearly to the shoulder. Even part of my face was in the mud. I was holding my books up out of the mud with my right hand. My audience of toughs was laughing and shouting 'Nice suit, kid.'

"Humiliated to the core, I wanted to crawl out of the mud, run back to my car, slide in, and drive away. Bo came down the soaked walkway, looked at me struggling in the mud and said, 'Who are you, son?' 'Your Food Services of America produce salesman, here for your order.' With that, he turned to the laughing gallery, told them to shut up, and give me a hand into the building.

"Two big guys came down and lifted me up by my armpits (minus one shoe) and carried me, into the building. I began warming up by the big, hot, potbellied stove. Bo handed me a white cook's uniform and showed me where to clean up and change.

"When I came out, Bo was sitting at the table closest to the stove. He said, 'Son, after what you've been through, let's fill up your truck!'

"When we were about finished writing up the order, one of Bo's helpers came out with my suit and shoes cleaned and dry. I changed, thanked Bo from the bottom of my heart, and drove away with my first order. I was a salesman now!"

If it had not been for a compassionate guy named Bo, I probably would not have even stayed in the food business and surely not in sales. Because of Bo's *life sentence,* I've enjoyed food sales for nearly 43 years. Bo's big order and his caring concern was a *life sentence* for me.

I want you to erase the memories when you slipped and fell. We have all had them. I want you to remember, to see on the movie picture screen of your mind, the beautiful, joyous, and generous experiences of your life. You've had them. I know you have. Now I ask you to unearth who has been "Bo" in your life? Dig those memories up. Why? These memories will provide a firm footing. Don't live in the past, but learn from the past, to see more clearly how big you are and how much bigger you can be. This will move you out of the muck of your falls and it will set your feet on solid ground.

"My mother said to me,
'If you are a soldier, you will become a general;
if you are a monk, you will become Pope.'
Instead I was a painter and became Picasso."
Pablo Picasso

Spouse Speak

Declarations from those we love, our parents, and spouses carry even greater impact because we are more vulnerable with those we love. Their opinions matter to us. So we are open, transparent, we let our defense down. Their opinions matter more to us than a boss, teacher, or customer and certainly more than the stranger on the street.

In 1850, Nathaniel Hawthorne went home to tell his wife he had just been fired. Is he vulnerable at this moment? Does her response matter? She's about to give him a *life sentence.* Did she say "Why can't you ever do anything right?" Or "What's going to happen to us now?" No. She said, "Good, now you can write your book." "What do we live on in the meanwhile?" Hawthorne asked. His wife opened a drawer filled with money. "I always knew you are a man of genius," she said. "So I saved a little each week, and now I have enough to last for a year." Now he was fired up! Hawthorne used that year to write The Scarlet Letter, one of the great masterpieces of American literature.

Our choice in a partner—the person we are attracted to, the person who is attracted to us, the person we fall in love with—reflects our self-image. Our selection of a spouse in our open culture is limited not by class or caste, only by our own choices. The decision we make when choosing our life partner is a reflection of our self-image. The *life sentences* you received in your earlier formative years influence your judgment when choosing your mate.

Our spouse reflects back to us their own self-image. And so those reflective comments they give us, those *life sentences,* spring from their self-view. If you are fortunate and fall in love with someone who has a strong self-image and healthy self-esteem, it will be easier for them to reinforce you in positive ways. The amplified impact of those we love is inescapable. We're most vulnerable and impressionable with those we love. Our relationship is a creative exchange where our unfolding self-concept continues to evolve.

"The supreme happiness of life
is the conviction of being loved for yourself,
or more correctly, being loved in spite of yourself."
Victor Hugo

Counselor

Linda, the student employment coordinator at a private college, told us: "One year before my husband, George, unexpectedly passed away, I arrived home to find him pacing the floor. My first thought was concern that something had happened to one of our three grown children. I asked, 'Is something wrong?' He approached me with expectation on his face and said, 'Everything is fine, I'm just having some problems at work. I value your opinion so much, I could hardly wait for you to come home to discuss it with you.'

"I told him he had just given me the greatest compliment any woman could ever receive. In the years since he has been gone, I've often drawn on that statement. It has given me the strength to know that I have good judgment and can make the right decisions! Even though I miss him and sometimes feel alone, his words ring in my ears to give me reassurance.

"The lesson I learned from this experience is that every word has the power to build someone's character, confidence, courage and self-esteem, or tear them down, dismiss, belittle, or even humiliate them."

Too often, the *life sentences* spouses give each other are negative, limiting, and restrictive, like "You never think ahead." "You never listen." "I've never seen anyone so lazy." On the other hand, when our spouse says, "You are always so thoughtful, understanding, creative, careful," the impact is inescapable, these *life sentences* stick. The highest purpose of marriage is to help our partner discover their unique strengths and reach more of their true potential. The best marriages are punctuated with constructive, empowering *life sentences.*

"Changing what you have comes from changing who you are. And changing who you are comes from changing what you think."

Mike Dooley

Bashing and Boosting Bosses

How do our bosses give us *life sentences*? In the first chapter I cited several examples from my own life of the impact bosses made with a few words. The point is simply this: anyone in authority can easily impact us with their *life sentence*. Our bosses, coaches, teachers have authority over us, and are with us through stretching times –vulnerable times. Bosses, coaches and senior coworkers are there when we are stretched outside of our comfort zone and receptive to suggestions. The feedback we hear at these vulnerable times can permanently influence our view of our selves. This feedback, these *life sentences*, help to determine the course, the direction of our careers and lives. We decide on our career path: management, go back to school, change direction, or go into business for ourselves. Big decisions that affect the rest of our lives.

Employee of the Year

Dani, expediter for Cascade Corporation in Springfield, Ohio, told us: "In February of 1991, I was living in Michigan and working as a receptionist for the Rittal Company. After about six months, I was offered an inside sales position. I was shocked and told my manager that I didn't feel qualified. I didn't have a college degree or any sales experience. My manager had complete confidence in me and persuaded me to take the position. Even though I had my manager's support, I didn't enjoy the support of the outside sales person, the regional manager, or president of the company. I knew from the beginning that everyone's eyes would be on me. I was going to have to prove myself. I left Rittal one Friday evening as a receptionist and the next Monday morning, came to work as an inside sales rep. I had no training whatsoever before being put behind a desk with a computer and phone. I started taking calls before I even knew how to check stock and enter an order.

My best phone phrase was, "I'm sorry. I don't know the answer to your question. I will find out and call you back today." I always called customers back the same day even if I didn't have an answer just so they knew I hadn't forgotten them.

"Within a year, I built close relationships with many customers and my outside sales rep. I worked many long weekdays and Saturdays to keep up, both for my customers and to further develop my knowledge. After being in the inside sales position for about a year, I was asked to travel with my manager to the corporate office in Springfield, Ohio, to help conduct interviews for a new sales rep position. The corporate office was having an annual Christmas luncheon for almost 300 people. As a part of the luncheon program, the president of Rittal gave out awards, including Employee of the Year, First Runner Up, and Second Runner Up. When my name was announced for First Runner Up, my stomach turned upside down. Tears drenched my face as I shook the President's hand and accepted the award. It had been one of the most challenging and difficult times of my life, but I did it. My outside sales rep believed in me. From the beginning my regional manager said, 'I believe in you.' He would never let me give up on myself. He was always there with the life affirming *life sentence*, 'You can do this."
We make important decisions because of the influence of these powerful people that determine our future. In large measure, all of these decisions are determined by the impact of the *life sentence* we are given by others and certainly, our coaches and bosses play a major role in our decision-making process. We never make these life-changing career choices in a vacuum.

"If we let things terrify us, life will not be worth living."
Seneca

Take Charge Guy

Bud Hogeberg gave me many *life sentences* when, at age 26, I started in the training business. I was on the phone making cold calls. I can still feel his hand on my shoulder as he rushed by, saying, "Larry, you are going to be a great success because you don't waste any of your precious time." Even though I was scared to death, I pressed forward, making more and more phone calls. When Bud arrived to teach the first session of a sales class I'd sold to the Northwest Board of Realtors in Lavonia, Michigan, I was setting up chairs and properly arranging the room. He gave me a *life sentence* when he said, "You're going to be a great success in this business because you are a take-charge guy."

Over the following year my wife, Donna Lee, and I struggled to make ends meet on straight commission. I watched several people give up and move on including the guy who hired me. Bud's *life sentences* gave me the courage to stick it out.

"The brave man is not he who does not feel afraid,
but he who conquers that fear."
Nelson Mandela

Author

Without Dick Morgul, my regional manager from Garden City, New York, you wouldn't be reading this book right now. In 1973, he gave me a powerful *life sentence* when he said, "Larry, when are you going to write your book?" My first thought was, "Me? Never." But the idea continued to rattle around in my head and heart. My first book, Repeat Business: 6 Steps to Superior Customer Service, was published 19 years later in 1992. The book you are reading is my eleventh book. I am not sure I would have written one page if it had not been for Dick's *life sentence.*

Dimensions

Ralph Nichols, president of the Nichols Corporation, gave me many *life sentences.* One I remember well was after Ralph heard my talk, "Time, A New Dimension" as part of our Friday weekly team meeting. He said, "Someday your talk will be more popular than the Success Triangle presentation." At that time I was part of the world's largest adult education organization and the "Success Triangle" was the most popular talk given by hundreds of the leaders.

"A candle loses nothing by lighting another candle."
Erin Majors

Gold Medal

Michael Phelps competed in six swimming events at the 2016 Summer Olympics. He won five gold medals, and one silver in the 100-meter butterfly. Joseph Schooling won the gold medal in that event.

In 2008, ahead of the Beijing Olympics, Michael Phelps showed up at the club where Joseph trained. While other kids rushed at Phelps wanting photos, Joseph was frozen. He couldn't believe his swimming idol was standing in front of him. Eventually, the 13-year-old mustered up the courage to ask for a picture.

Four years later in 2012, when making his Olympic debut, Joseph's swim cap and goggles were rejected for not meeting Olympic regulations. Michael noticed the dejected young man, hugged him, and said, "You're so young, you still have a long way to go. It's a learning experience so keep your head high and just keep moving on."

Later at the medalists' news conference, Phelps urged reporters to ask Joseph some questions. "I'm proud of Joe," Phelps said. "I've been able to watch him grow and turn into the swimmer that he is." Joseph said, "A lot of this is because of Michael. He's the reason why I want to be a better swimmer."

The highest purpose of a leader is to create leaders who exceed their accomplishments. Your *life sentences* help create your replacement. The person who will carry the torch when you move on. The point of this story is that the more successful you are, the more impact you have with others, and the more receptive they are to the declarations you make. The real purpose for being "a winner" who is respected is to have maximum influence with as many others as possible to help them reach their true potential. They stand on your shoulders.

Remember the *life sentences* that feed your soul, that you resonate with, that support you, that give you a sense of power, that cause you to sit up in your chair, and to stand up straight. Listen to those declarations that help you believe in yourself, believe in your dreams. Listen to those declarations that help you lead from strength and build your sense of self-worth.

"When we become more fully aware that our success is due in large measure to the loyalty, helpfulness, and encouragement we have received from others, our desire grows to pass on similar gifts. Gratitude spurs us on to prove ourselves worthy of what others have done for us. The spirit of gratitude is a powerful energizer."

Wilferd Peterson

Now write down *life sentences* that helped you believe in your potential and see yourself as bigger than you had ever believed before. Please do it now!

Write down a few of the powerful, positive *life sentences* your <u>parents</u> or <u>parental figures</u> gave you.

Write down one or more of the positive *life sentences* <u>friends</u> or <u>loved ones</u> gave you.

Use this space to write down any of the powerful, positive *life sentences* your <u>teachers</u>, <u>bosses</u>, or <u>coaches</u> gave you.

You have a story. I know you do. Your story has many chapters. Someone believed in you and told you so. Please do not turn this page until you have written down a few brief notes about at least three of your positive *life sentences.* Now enjoy the positive feelings remembering evokes.

Chapter Two

"It is one of the most beautiful compensations of life that no man can sincerely try to help another without helping himself."
Ralph Waldo Emerson

YOU BE THE JUDGE

We have seen the power of good judgments and the *life sentence* effect they can have. Now let's look at your power to make good judgments, to declare *life sentences* for others.

You are being called to a great life purpose. There is no greater purpose, no greater calling than to empower others on their life's journey. You fulfill this purpose by helping others see themselves in the light of their strengths. As you respond to this call, you both stand tall.

"Give so much time to the improvement of yourself that you have no time to criticize others."
Christian D. Larson

Picasso

Becky, retail manager for a world-class truck plaza, told us: "In September of 1995, I received a call from a friend in Cabo San Lucas, Mexico. She asked if I could come and help some kids who really needed help. It only took me seconds to answer 'Yes.' I gave notice at work and I put everything I owned into storage. I kissed my family and friends goodbye and headed for the unknown.

"When I walked into the rundown trailer that was now our classroom, I saw fifteen of the most beautiful little faces I had ever seen. It was love at first sight! Their ages ranged from nine to seventeen. These were angry, broken kids who didn't care about anyone or anything. Not one of them knew their self-worth. So I began teaching what turned out to be a three-year healing school and they began to blossom into young people who liked and respected themselves.

"My biggest challenge was the seventeen-year-old boy, A.J. Confused, lost, nowhere to go, he told me he didn't respect or trust anyone. I told him, "That's okay because I will earn your trust and respect." So that's where our story began. Soon he wanted to come to school. He started actively participating. He was the most naturally talented artist I had ever seen. We developed a strong bond. His parents didn't believe he'd ever amount to anything. Finally with a lot of work, I convinced them to take the time to really look at their son and begin to believe in him.

"Now AJ works as an artist in Orlando, Florida for Disney Studios. I hear from him frequently. He emailed me a while back to ask if I would please come to his June wedding. He said he'd like me to be there so I could witness the difference I made in his life.

"The lesson I learned from this experience is how powerful my belief and words of encouragement can be. I learned firsthand that I can decree *life sentences* that change others for the rest of their lives."

For you to even approximate your potential for liberating others with *life sentences*, you must overcome one of our most natural tendencies, the natural tendency to be a fault-finder, a speck-spotter, a chip-checker. You must force yourself to look past the obvious imperfections people are already aware of, often painfully aware of, and instead see their powerful potential, the hidden wholeness that is sometimes just below the flaw. There is a part of us that seems to think we are out of integrity if we give a compliment to a person who isn't perfect. We think pointing out a strength without being sure the receiver knows we also saw their foibles and shortcomings is dishonest. For you to realize your potential for changing others' lives for the better, you finally come to the place where you trust that people will discover soon enough their weaknesses. They really don't require your expertise to help them find their faults. And you must come at last to believe that the greatest gift you can offer another is the gift of observing and pointing out their strengths, helping them see, helping them discover their perfection and potential.

You might wonder, "How can I go around trying to inspire others, trying to empower them, when I don't feel so empowered myself?" When you make a decision to see how many people you can awaken to their strengths and potential, an amazing thing happens. You discover that as you empower others with your words of encouragement, your declared *life sentence*, you receive a carbon copy of the blessing you gave them. Your empowering *life sentences* have a way of becoming a boomerang, and the more boomerangs you throw, the more come back to you.

Never underestimate how far reaching your impact can be. Sometimes just touching one person will have a ripple effect that impacts thousands. We really don't understand the workings of the universe, the influence of the ripple effect of the flap of the butterfly wing. Take advantage of your power to touch the lives of others and leave the results to themselves. Slowly, imperceptibly at first, you'll begin to change. You'll begin to see yourself differently. Like a snake, you'll shed your skin. Like a lobster you'll lose your limiting shell. You'll reinvent yourself.

I challenge you to awaken at least one person a day to a little more of their potential. Praise an unrecognized strength, delegate more responsibility, ask their thoughts, and as often as possible use their ideas and give them the credit.

You may find your greatest challenge is praising those who rub you the wrong way. How could you sincerely praise a person you dislike? This will probably push you out of your comfort zone and calls for wise discernment. I am not suggesting you praise anyone for things that aren't true. In fact, for your praise to create a life-changing *life sentence* it must be based on the whole truth, the impeccable truth. For your *life sentence* to have a positive, life-changing impact, it must be the truth about a specific, observable quality like creativity, organization, patience, or determination. Your *life sentences* must be backed up by an observed behavior that demonstrates and proves the praised strength. Since this person knows there has been friction and distance between you, your encouraging compliment will be more powerful. You may create more of a *life sentence* impact than you would if they were one of your close friends. You could, literally, turn their life around, set them on a new trajectory. The only question that remains is can you bring yourself to do it? Can you set aside your ego, your need to be right, your need to get even, long enough to observe those behaviors that reveal their strength and declare the *life sentence* they deserve?

"Forgive yourself for your faults and mistakes and move on."
Les Brown

Oops

Bonnie, a design engineer for Cascade Corporation, told us: "When I first started working at Cascade Corporation as a typist back in 1973, almost twenty-five years ago, each purchase order was typed and given to the buyer for approval and a signature. When a requisition became a purchase order, the delivery address was then typed on the form.

"I was new and I really wanted to make a good impression. I went to work typing a huge stack of purchase orders on my desk. I whipped out the entire pile in no time. Then I presented them to my supervisor for her signature. My first impression of her had been she was a rather stern lady.

"Shortly after I handed her the stack of orders, she called me back to her desk. I was so nervous my palms broke out in a sweat, there was a dryness in my throat, and my heart started racing. My mind stormed through all of the tasks I had accomplished that day, searching for something I had done wrong that could have displeased her.

"When I sat down at her desk, she told me with a little side-smile that she thought it might be wise if I were to change the delivery address on one of my purchase orders to Whittenberg with a 'W', instead of Whittenberg with an 'S.' Boy, was my face red!!"

This is a wonderful story of a young woman who wanted to do her best—a person dedicated to contributing, wanted to be productive, and in the process, made an honest mistake. Her boss did not find it necessary to laugh at her mistake or tell others what she had done wrong. All she did was smile as she gave Bonnie an opportunity to correct the error.

The role of an empowering leader is to find ways to build people and make them successful. Discover ways to help team members save face when they blow it, make those inevitable mistakes. Take every opportunity to create positive *life sentences* and you will improve morale and create empowered team members who take responsibility for their errors and mistakes. You will develop a team that is committed to taking the risks required for making continuous improvement. A team willing to risk for the sake of progress, growth, and advancement. Unless you create courageous individuals, you will be in the deep doo-doo of the "also-rans," not one of the championship teams that win repeatedly.

"Example is not the main thing in influencing others, it's the only thing"
Albert Schweitzer

Just Kidding Around

We all have influence with the children in our lives. We influence them with the *life sentences* we declare.

In spite of our great intentions, we all make mistakes with kids. If you made mistakes with the children in your life, join the human race. It's not the purpose of this book to criticize your efforts. We've all made mistakes in our role as parents, god parents, and grandparents. Let's go on from where we are.

Most preschoolers hear far more put downs, don'ts, cant's, and other limiting feedback than they hear positive, encouraging, praising comments like, "Good job!" "Thank you!" "Atta boy." "You are the best." A UCLA survey from a decade ago reported the average one-year-old child hears the word, "no" more than 400 times a day! At first, you may think this must be an exaggeration but consider this. When we tell a toddler "No" we usually say, "No, no, no!" That is three times in three seconds! Another study estimates the average child hears the word "No" or "Don't" over 148,000 times while growing up, compared with just a few thousand "Yes" messages.

When we say, "I told you a thousand times," it literally is true. We have limited, disempowered, put our children down thousands of times. Each time we say, "When will you ever learn?" "Can't you do anything right?" "How many times do I have to tell you?" "You did it again." "That's not the right way." "You are so bashful, shy, slow, or clumsy." "You always make such a mess." "Look what you did this time." "Will you stop that?" These are destructive phrases. As they accumulate, they can define who your child thinks they are, what they will attempt in the future, and who they will be.

With determination, turn this practice around. This change, like all change, requires self-awareness, effort, and discipline. Break free from your own parents' modeling and establish patterns that are unlike many common parenting practices.

You can say, "That was great." "You are so neat." "I love your enthusiasm." "Thanks for caring and sharing." "You just keep getting better." "I sure like the way you think." "You are a smart one." "Thanks for picking it up." "You are always improving things."

To practice this approach to parenting requires creativity, enthusiasm, and innovation. You must know and understand that there really are two ways to describe most events – "half-empty" versus "half-full." Somehow we feel we are helping our children by pointing out their faults and failings, when in fact, in many cases, they are already painfully aware of their misses. We help them far more by pointing out and highlighting their strengths, their successes, their achievements, their victories, and their progress. By celebrating progress and advancement, by pointing out their strengths instead of the glaring weaknesses, you help them grow.

Let me add that I am not talking about lowering your

standard or being an enabling parent who makes excuses for our children's inappropriate behavior. In fact, I believe that you must set high standards, have high expectations, and when discipline is called for, and it will be, be consistent in applying discipline. You can do this and perhaps find more opportunity for positive *life sentences* than those parents who shout, complain, and grumble. When standards are violated, be a parent of a few stern words and certain disciplines. Keep the content and tone of your relationship filled with passionate, uplifting *life sentences.*

This approach to parenting requires a confident, centered parent. The best things we can do for our children is to provide an example of competent, humble love and assurance which will help them develop a strong self-image, great self-esteem, and greater self-confidence.

"It is time for us all to stand and cheer for the doer, the achiever – the one who recognizes the challenges and does something about it."
Vince Lombardi

Bump on the Head

James, foreman for a plumbing contractor in Battle Ground, Washington, told us: "When we were assigned the 'Pearl Project' (a person you want to improve your relationship with), I chose my son, Seth.

"Seth was five-years-old when he fell off a deck. A life-flight helicopter took him to a children's hospital. He suffered a concussion and as a result suffered setbacks in his learning ability.

"We have been to many doctors trying to get help for him. Teachers have pushed him through the system. His schoolwork has been terrible. He never brought any homework home and never once got above a 'C' in class.

"About six months ago my wife and I went to a psychiatrist. The psychiatrist thought we were expecting too much from him. A week after the Pearl Project was assigned, my wife and I started to praise him for the smallest things. We would ask permission to provide input. When he said 'Yes,' 'Sure,' or 'I guess' we'd tell him a small way he could improve, and predict a positive outcome. It was like a light bulb turned on. Suddenly, his schoolwork became more important to him. He brought his homework home and asked my wife to help him. His attention to projects at home is much better than it has ever been. Using Turbo's 15 Leadership Principles puts an entirely new meaning into teaching our children.

The lesson I learned is that I should never give up on anyone. There is always potential deep inside, and positive attention, followed by encouragement can help find it. They may surprise me someday. Maybe not today, but one day they will."

You can change the course of someone's life with well-timed, encouraging feedback. I want you to get enthusiastic about changing people's lives for the better with the power of your verbalized observations, the life sentence only you can give. I want you to get excited about the power your spoken word has to change people's direction or help speed them along in the direction they are headed.

"It's not a proper feedback if it's given
to flatter and/or belittle someone.
True feedback should be given
to empower someone to perform better."
Assegid Habtewold

Coach Dan

Dan, senior project manager for a fifty-year-old excavation contractor in Salem, Oregon, told us: "In the spring of 2010, my wife and I were at home in Canby, Oregon with our two sons eating dinner and discussing baseball tryouts from the week before. We had been involved with youth sports since our boys were old enough to play and I had assisted coaching at some level when time allowed.

"In years past we would receive a phone call from the coach telling us what team our son had been selected to play on. Tonight's call was different, the head of the youth program told me there weren't enough coaches for the teams at our oldest son, Cole's, level. Then he asked if I wanted to coach. At first, I said 'No, I am too busy to make that full time commitment.' He said, 'If you don't, I'm afraid there won't be any one to coach Cole's team.' I asked Matt, another dad, if we could split coaching duties and he agreed. Now, we had to 'draft' our team. Nick, one of the boys we considered drafting, was a good baseball player but he had an attitude problem. We decided to go ahead and select Nick for our team.

"As the season progressed there were a few problems, such as tardiness to practice, some attitude, and doing what he thought was best during games, not what was best for the team. Nick seemed to respond to the coaching that Matt and I provided, whether it was reprimanding him or complimenting him, he just liked the attention. During the season, I noticed he didn't have family show up to watch his games. I thought this might be the reason for his behavior. The more positive reinforcement we gave him, the harder Nick tried and the less he acted out.

"Although I only coached Nick for one year, he and my son played on the same teams and I saw him often. He was always respectful and called me 'Coach Dan.' A few times he texted to see if I had watched him play football or seen him at the last baseball game. I remember seeing him running stairs and sprinting by himself preparing for the upcoming season. I told him how impressed I was with his work ethic and proud of the man he had become.

"At the high school graduation awards ceremony, I was excited to learn that Nick had received a wrestling scholarship. As I walked out of the auditorium, I saw Nick in the parking lot; he made a point of walking over to shake my hand, giving me a hug, and asking if I had seen he won a scholarship. This made the little time I had invested in youth coaching highly rewarding. The lesson I learned from this experience is I can have a life-changing impact with well-timed coaching and encouragement. I can hit a 'home run' with my team by providing coaching, encouragement, and praise.

Pick an area you would like to see the young people in your world grow, the behavior you would like to see them take on, a quality you would like to see more of in their life. Now develop a strategy. What can you say, how can you give them a life sentence that will help them be more of this kind of person? Remember, you are influencing not only the next generation, you are affecting the ones that follow. The *life sentences* you declare will be passed on to the next generations. For most of us, this positive approach will require work, effort and personal discipline. Isn't it interesting we are more comfortable giving criticism than we are praising. Pointing out and emphasizing strengths will be work and requires effort. It won't be easy or natural, and you may feel awkward. The stretch, the effort, will be worth it.

If you want to be great, see the greatness in others. Holding a vision of greatness for them is a path to discovering the greatness in yourself.

One of the precious gifts you can bring every person you meet is to see their essence. Don't just see people as their surface personality. Don't see them as their history, what they look like physically, or see them as a title or position. Instead, begin the practice of seeing their heart. It might be the highest practice of your day. Practice seeing their true beauty. Practice seeing a great soul in their amazing human flesh disguise. In this seeing, you are actually helping anchor heaven on earth. By this seeing, you are strengthening the one in front of you, behind you, beside you, those around you, and certainly that person inside you. This is a win-win-win spiritual practice. They win, you win, and all of the earth wins because the world is better each time one of us rises to a higher vibration. Seeing the other persons potential is the first step. Declaring a life sentence is where you leverage this seeing and take it to a completely new level. Change their life as you add new purpose to yours.

"There is no greater joy nor greater reward than to make a fundamental difference in someone's life."
Sister May Rose McGeady

See Other's Point of View

Jerome, superintendent for a general contractor in Battle Ground, Washington, told us: "My second son Kai is a unique person; Kai has a different way of communicating and responding to those around him. Doctors and therapists have given him several different diagnoses but I am still not sure if any of them really fit.

"A few days after the third session of the Leadership Development Lab I was heading home from work when my wife called and told me that Kai had made a mistake and I couldn't be mad at him. When I got home, Kai was crying in his room because he knew I was going to be angry with him because he had ruined our phone charger.

"This made me think to use Leadership Principle # 5: 'See things from the other persons' point of view.' If I were frustrated about something and needed help learning how to deal with it, how would it feel to have my father mad at me? I realized that most of my communication with Kai was about problems, things that were not going well. So, I started to listen more to him, find positive things to compliment him on and positive things that we could just talk about.

"A couple of weeks ago we had to have a discussion about his lack of follow through on bringing his homework back and forth from school. He knows that this is his responsibility. Rather than just telling him that he needs to get better or bad things will happen. I asked him what we could do to help him remember to be more responsible with his homework. We talked for a while and both decided that he needed a chart that he could check off when he completed his homework. When we finished talking about his 'performance chart,' I could see a twinkle in his eye, so I asked what he was thinking. He said 'Dad what do you think I would get if I filled the chart out?'

"I said, 'So you're trying to get something out of dad now?' We started laughing.

"This helped me realize how changing my way of talking to him, just a little bit, has led to much more progress than I had ever seen in the past. Eliminating the 3C's, Don't Criticize, Condemn, or Complain (Leadership Principle #3), Be An Active Listener (Leadership Principle #6), and giving him a way to track positive progress are small changes in me, that have had a huge impact on Kai.

"The lesson I learned is that helping my son be successful is far more important than just being 'right' – I want my son and others to be successful.

"The action I call you to take is to use all 15 of the Leadership Principles in small and big ways to change the way you interact with the people around you. When you do, you help them want to do, what you want them to do."

You are not diminished by giving praise, by recognizing the strengths of another. You don't lose a part of yourself when you give a compliment, affirm someone, give a life sentence to another. On the contrary, you grow in stature in your own eyes and in the eyes of others.

You can be an artist with your words, with caring, genuine interest in others, and through the process help create a masterpiece.

So, this is your path, your path to the purpose and fulfillment we all naturally desire. It isn't seeking happiness. Instead, it is exercising compassion as we seek to help others in finding their true selves and experience greater purpose and fulfillment in their lives.

"The best way to cheer yourself up – cheer everybody else up."
Mark Twain

Leave the 3C's Behind (Criticize, Condemn, Complain)

Robbie, foreman for a plumbing company in Battle Ground, Washington, told us: "This past spring and summer my family and I were building our new home in Hockinson, WA. I knew it would be a big job. I was planning to do a lot of the work myself with the help of friends and family. My oldest son Derek was a junior and I was counting on him for much of the help I would need. It didn't go so well. The way I saw it he always had an excuse for being late. When he was there, I felt he didn't do his part of the job that well. I could tell he really wanted to be somewhere else with his friends. It got so bad I became so disgusted that I didn't even want him to help. I have always heard what a hard worker he is and it pissed me off because he wouldn't work that hard helping me. Before the house was finished, I started ignoring my son because all we would do was argue. He wanted to move out, and I couldn't wait for him to graduate so he'd get out.

"After starting the Leadership Development Lab (LDL), I chose Derek as my pearl, a father and son's relationship shouldn't be this way. I realized that my disgust had become so bad that every time I looked at him it was with a 3C's (Criticize, Condemn, and Complain) label. I was looking for anything wrong I could find to help reinforce my feelings. And looking back, I now realize, he sensed it.

"Over the past month, we haven't had a lot of interaction because we are both busy. Instead of ignoring him as I had been, I've asked simple questions and listened. I abandoned the 3C's and things are much better now.

"The lesson I learned is not to get stuck on the 3C's. They are detrimental to my relationships."

A week later Robbie gave me an update on his story, "After I gave this presentation at the LDL I was still feeling that maybe I hadn't been trying hard enough. When I got home after 10 pm, I saw my son for the first time that day. It was late but I asked him how his day was and listened. It was a brief conversation. About an hour later as he was heading for bed, he said something I haven't heard for a long time. 'Good night dad, love you.'

"Before that moment I thought I'd have to move a mountain. But that night I realized I had already moved that mountain, pebble by pebble."

If you dedicate yourself to the task of enlivening everyone you meet, liberating your family, friends, and associates, you will be alert and stay awake all day, every day. Make a game of it. See how often you can catch people in the act of playing hide and seek from their greatness. Be on the alert for the little risks people take. Pay special attention to the things they seem unsure of, afraid of or tentative about. The times they try something new, do something in a different way, stretch beyond their comfort zone, exercise that most valuable of all human traits – courage. Watch for examples of determination, initiative, decisiveness, insightfulness, creativity, and ingenuity. Look for any of the positive qualities that, when employed, are liberating and lead to greater self-expression and fulfillment.

When you ignore those around you, when you fail to notice their efforts, their challenges, their creativity, their determination, their interests, their caring, it's almost as if you are punishing them. Certainly, you missed an opportunity, possibly an opportunity of a lifetime to provide *life sentences*, to awaken them to a strength they may never fully see without your alert, verbalized observation of the quality beneath their performance.

Doing this will require mental effort. You will have to think. Accept my challenge to exercise your power of making liberating *life sentences* that empower others to live at a higher level. A level that more closely matches their limitless potential. Sharpen your skills of observation, discernment and awareness of the good that is going on all around you.

"To the world you might be one person,
but to one person, you might be the world."
Taylor Hanson

Thirty Years Later

After graduation, I took a job with the W. Bingham Company, a 100-year-old wholesale hardware business in, what was for me, the huge city of Cleveland, Ohio. Moving to Cleveland was outside my comfort zone. I knew no one in the area, was earning very little money, and I had no place to live. I lived at the YMCA for a few days. That was an experience. The Nactigals, my minister and his wife, invited me to move into the third floor room above the parsonage. The predominantly German congregation still conducted their Wednesday night services in German. I was active in the church youth group. Reverend Sam Nactigal and I went to hear a "positive thinking" speaker one evening. As we drove home, he asked my impressions. I didn't hold back. My views were more trusting, than Rev. Sam's, of the positive possibility the speaker had spoken about.

I was an energetic 19-year-old who created plenty of commotion in the house. I'm sure the first time I drove my 1932 Ford hot rod in and parked it in my space beside their garage they were a little shocked.

I only lived with them for about a year. We had little contact after I left to for the Army. Through a series of almost indescribable coincidences, my wife, Donna Lee, and I met Sam in his wheelchair some 30 years later in Tigard, OR. As we were being reacquainted, I was blown away when he took out his billfold and showed a picture of me he'd been carrying all those years. I can only conclude somehow I had a *life sentence* impact on Reverend Sam.

How do you give a *life sentence* that stays, a *life sentence* that sticks, a *life sentence* that pays off in the other person seeing himself or herself differently, seeing themselves as more than how they have been defining themselves?

First, you must sharpen your skills of observation. Look beyond the way you may have come to define them in terms of their shortcomings, weaknesses, and faults. Watch closely for an instance when they demonstrate a quality you would like to see more often.

Second, tell them - you must speak up. When you see a positive quality like one of these...

Accountable
Accurate
Appreciative
Articulate
Assertive
Confident
Conscientious
Considerate
Consistent
Constructive
Creative
Dependable
Diligent
Disciplined
Efficient
Flexible
Focused
Genuine
Gracious
Helpful
Initiative
Inspirational
Intelligent
Listening
Logical
Methodical
Observant
Organized
Patient
Polite
Positive
Proactive
Reliable
Respectful
Responsive
Sincere
Systematic
Tactful
Teachable
Trustworthy
Understanding
Versatile
Visionary
Wise

...follow the guidelines on page 55:

Read the following illustrations to hear how *life sentences* might sound:

"Marie, you are so creative! The way you video your kids in city parks and then post their reviews online. As you continue to apply your creativity to project bids our win rate of profitable jobs will improve."

"Alan, you demonstrate so much courage when you step into a karate tournament ring! As you apply that same courage on contract change order disputes your success is guaranteed."

"Frank, you showed amazing determination! The way you studied eight long years for your chiropractor's degree! This is the kind of determination that insures the successful growth of your practice."

A. Start with their name, "*Harry*..."

B. Now name the quality you saw. Don't say *"I think"* – make an active declaration. Example: insightful *"...you showed great insight."*

C. Now spell out what they did that proves the quality, *"Your careful thought on how to approach our key supplier is why we got preferred treatment."* Pause for a second to be sure they see it.

D. Then say, *"AS you* (not IF) *continue to show great insight you will bring this project in ahead of schedule."* Say no more - zip your lip.

Praise creates *life sentences* when it awakens the receiver to an awareness of an unrecognized strength.

Giving a *life sentence* is an intimate exchange between two people. Must I say it? Of course, you must be honest. You must be sincere.

What still may need to be said is this, your *life sentence* doesn't mean the person is perfect. It doesn't mean they demonstrate this valuable quality all the time or even often. They don't – who does?

It does mean that for once you stopped long enough, were perceptive enough, aware enough to see this spark of perfection and you were courageous enough to tell them what you saw. You said it without reserve, without holding back, and without the qualifiers of "I think" or "if."

One last thing, this is not my formula. I cannot, do not claim originality with it. It is the formula many of our dads, moms, coaches, and bosses used with us – except they used it in reverse. They used it backward. They used it to tear down, not to build up.

They started by calling you by name, as I did when I really wanted to get my son's attention. (Sometimes they might have even included your middle name.) Then they followed with a defining negative quality like sloppy, lazy, careless, stupid, uncoordinated, slow, impatient, mean, dishonest.

They said, *"__Your name__, you are so _negative quality_. Look at the way you just ____did or said something______."* (The proof that you should be labeled with the above negative quality.) They ended with, *"You keep that ____negative quality____ up and you will never amount to a hill of beans!"*

Chapter Three

"The purpose of life is for the individual to become greater than the definitions he has inherited."
James Baldwin

Jail Break

Get Out of Jail Free

Remember the Monopoly "Get Out of Jail Free" card? Wouldn't it be great if you had a "Get Out of Jail Free" card that would allow you to escape the negative *life sentences*, escape all the limiting cells you inherited?

There are only 50 governors and one President in the United States who can pardon a literal life in prison sentence. If you are waiting for one of the "51" people, whoever they happen to be in your life, to commute your *life sentences*, you're going to wait too long. You and you alone must take the necessary steps to commute your negative *life sentences*.

The pages that follow will reveal how you can commute your *life sentences* and set yourself free. Imagine what it would be like for someone who had been sentenced to life in prison to discover they didn't have to wait for the President of the United States or their state's Governor to commute their life sentence? Rather than waiting for someone else to repeal their life sentence, all the prisoner had to do was call the Warden and say the word. One phone call and they would be free.

The good news is you have that power. You have the power to commute any limiting *life sentences* you were given that are holding you back.

Reinforcing your positive *life sentences* will earn your early release. Earning a pardon from your negative *life sentences* will take sincere effort. It may not come overnight. There is no quick pardon, no single magic word. As you persist in applying the ideas in this and the next chapter you will experience a greater sense of liberty and incremental increases in your freedom every day until you are completely free.

"If someone talked to you the way you talk to yourself, you would have kicked them out of your life long ago."
Carla Gordan

Self-Sentences

Self-sentences are the most powerful sentences of all. The most powerful *life sentences* ever uttered are what you say to yourself about yourself. Remember, words, even silently spoken, create pictures, pictures create emotions, and emotions create motion. Awareness of what you are saying to yourself about yourself is one of the most important parts of your program for shortening your sentence and earning your pardon.

Most of us give ourselves several *life sentences* every day. How? In the same way, others give us *life sentences*. We tell ourselves who we are, what we can and cannot do. We say things like "I could never do that!" Listen to the certainty, the strength, and ownership in that pronouncement. Who "couldn't"? You couldn't. And when couldn't you? Never!

As Richard Bock says in *Illusions, "Argue for your limitations and they are yours."* I've heard people say, "That's just the way I am." "That's the way I've always been." "My whole family is that way." As if, the behavior trait is somehow embedded in their DNA. As if that limitation were cast in bronze. They own the limitation. They hold title to their weaknesses, flaws, shortcomings that they convincingly argue for.

Maybe you say, "I just can't help it." Then use ethnic roots or family of origin to justify your shortcomings while reinforcing your self-imposed *life sentence.* "What do you expect from me? I am Italian." "Oh, it's my German side coming out." "I have my grandmother's English dry wit." This is your excuse, the argument you use for your belittling, sarcastic remarks. With these declarative statements, you reinforce and perpetuate the sentences given to you by others.

About ten years ago, my wife and I turned this limiting practice of owning weaknesses and shortcomings around. We started playing a fun little game. When I give her a compliment, or she me, we never reply "Not really" "I didn't think it was that good" "What do you want from me now." Instead, we say "Thank you." Then we argue for our strengths, our strong suits by saying, "That's the way I have always been, in fact my whole family is that way." We love this game and recommend it to you. Put a positive spin on your DNA and your heritage. Instead of arguing for your weaknesses, argue for your strengths.

"Wanting to be someone else is a waste of the person you are."

Kurt Cobain

Thank Me

I wish you could listen to the voice in my head. I say "Thank you" under my breath dozens, maybe 100's of times every day.

May I be personal for a moment longer? The magazines you pass in the grocery checkout line like *People Magazine, National Enquirer,* and *O, The Oprah Magazine* are there to encourage you to live vicariously through the lives of others.

I include in my daily morning ritual this simple prayer, "Thank you God that I am Larry Dennis." I mean it. I am glad to be me with all of my family of origin flaws, my weaknesses, shortcomings, and inadequacies. I am glad to be me. I never wish, in the smallest way, to be someone else. When you can say "Thank you *(fill in your full birth name)*" regardless of your circumstances, you will be free.

"Nothing splendid has ever been achieved except by those who dared believe that something inside of them was superior to circumstance."
Bruce Barton

Back to School

Deborah, office manager of a medical equipment distributor told us: "I had been active in our children's school and in the PTA for several years when I learned no one had filed for an open position on the school board. I immediately felt this was the perfect opportunity for me to become a meaningful part of the future of public education. I was a perfect candidate because of all the time and work I had invested as an active member of the PTA. When I asked my friends and associates to sign the petition for my candidacy, several expressed concerns at my lack of "social standing" in the community. After all, I didn't frequent the same circles as the present board members and Hillsboro seemed to them, to be a snobbish community. At one point, I was nearly convinced to drop the idea. The last thing I wanted was to look foolish, but I forged ahead, turned in the petition and got my name on the ballot.

"Running for office wasn't easy. Three men ran against me. The local newspaper made it obvious they thought I was the least able of the candidates. They interviewed all of us, but in the newspaper article, they quoted the men on important issues and me on the more trivial, lightweight subjects, such as playground equipment. It seemed to me they did everything they could to make me sound stupid and my opponents sound profound.

"In spite of what I felt was a strong bias on the part of the local newspaper, my efforts to reach voters worked and I won the election. I was honored to spend five years with four other capable, caring people who gave a great deal of their time and energy to the cause of public education. I met some of the most remarkable people in Oregon, including Norma Paulus, Oregon's Superintendent of Public Education, who attended the dedication of the new school I had the honor to help build.

"I will never forget the pride I felt as we toured Jackson school for the first time, and read the plaque with the names of all board members, including mine, in the entryway for everyone to see.

"The lesson I learned from this experience is some endeavors are too important to allow fear of failure to hold me back. It is not only the right, but also the obligation of every American to be involved with our local government. This is what our great country was built upon."

As you read this wonderful story did you see that the first election Deborah had to win was with herself? In her own mind, she had to be an elected one. She had to convince herself she was worthy of the position. She had to quiet the negative voice in the halls of her mind before she could see her name on the hallway plaque of the new Hillsboro school.

"Every problem has in it the seeds of its own solution.
If you don't have any problems, you don't get any seeds."
Norman Vincent Peale

Vega

Marshall, product development manager for a lift truck attachment company, told us: "Our product development team was into our project approximately three years when we learned the project could be canceled because the estimated cost of production would make the selling price exceed a price the market would bear. So we put the project on hold to do a cost reduction study. The study showed we could save more than $100 per unit if we changed from a steel sleeve cylinder construction to an anodized aluminum bore cylinder. This was a brand-new idea, a new paradigm. No one in our industry had ever used anodized aluminum hydraulic cylinders.

"As word spread around our company, several well-meaning 'advisers' and 'sidewalk foremen' stopped by my office to tell me 'we were crazy,' 'it wouldn't work,' and they reminded me of the ill-fated Vega engine. (The Vega was General Motor's first non-sleeved aluminum block engine. Unfortunately, for the unsuspecting car owner, this engine self-destructed after about 40,000 miles.)

"We forged on, contacted an anodizer, and asked them if they had done anything like this before. They hadn't but were sure they knew how to get it done. We took the risk and manufactured our hydraulic cylinders from anodized aluminum. On our quality test, we completed more than 530,000 prototype test cycles, with no leakage. Our original quality objective was only 50,000 cycles.

"What I learned from this experience is breaking out of the cells of past practices requires sound research and more than that I must stand up to the cheerleaders who predict my failure. I must be willing to take the risk of moving past conventional barriers. When I do, I am free to innovate, improve quality and I can reduce cost at the same time."

The path to freedom requires pressing beyond conventional thinking. Don't allow yourself to be a prisoner of the past. Just because a similar project didn't work 20 years ago, doesn't mean your innovative project, your new approach won't work today. Only breakout thinkers who take risks experience break throughs.

"I can feel guilty about the past, apprehensive about the future, but only in the present can I act."
Abraham Maslow

Performance Review

Ken, controller for a general contractor, told us: "It was 1989 and I was having my first performance evaluation with a northwest Portland furniture manufacturer. The president and I went out to lunch. I will never forget it. I remember the way he opened the manila folder. 'Ken,' he said, 'you're not making it as Controller. But this is a big job, so I am going to give you another three months.' I don't remember much of the rest of the day. Obviously, I was devastated and I didn't sleep much that night or any night for a long time. Never before in my life had I had to face failure. But, here I was, about to get fired because I wasn't good enough. I got down on my knees and let God know He had my attention. My mind went back to the seventh grade.

"Back in those days, they seemed to think it was important to give kids IQ tests, and I could hear my teacher and my Dad discussing the results of my test while I sat by silently. The bottom line, explained my teacher, was I was extremely normal, middle of the road, average – but I did try harder, which may account for getting good grades.

"I felt crushed I wanted to quit. Instead, I resolved to just try harder. It wasn't easy, there was no magic to it. The months that followed were stressful and I put in a lot of overtime. Three months came and went and I was still employed. Six months and still working hard. Eventually, the effort paid off. I began to feel at ease and I was promoted to Vice President.

"I recently left that company to take a new position. I had been there nearly ten years and made many good friends including the President.

"The lesson I learned from this experience is I don't need to be a genius to be successful. I just need to try harder than the person next in line for my position."

Your intelligence or lack of it are not the important factor in overcoming negative *life sentences.* In fact, greater intelligence can even get in the way. You can use your rational mind to justify, prove your negative *life sentences.* And Ken has reminded us that putting aside all of our negative *life sentences* will require hard work. The pay-off of breaking out, your newfound freedom is worth it!

"Happiness, knowledge, not in another place, but this place – nor for another hour, but this hour."
Walt Whitman

New York Minute

In the spring of 1976, as part of our ongoing training and development, my wife and I attended a speech workshop conducted in New York. After the Friday night session, Ollie, the president of the company I worked for asked, "Are you available for brunch Sunday morning?"

I said, "That would be wonderful."

"I'll send a car to pick you up."

For the next two days, I was a little nervous wondering what the brunch was all about. I had no idea why he was calling the meeting.

After being seated in one of the most beautiful restaurants I've ever eaten in, he said, "How do you like Rockford?"

My office had been there for a little over a year. Without hesitation I quickly said, "We love it."

His follow-up question was, "How much longer do you want to stay there?"

Again without hesitation, my response was, "Not a minute longer than I have to."

We had barely settled into our gorgeous home on the Rock River and I had just won the primary election for the Winnebago County Board. I meant it when I told him we loved it. And I was sincere when I said we were ready and eager to move on.

We moved from Birmingham, Michigan when I accepted the Rockford assignment only 18 months earlier. I was determined to put down deep roots quickly. I was elected to the Winnebago Hospital Planning Commission six months earlier. We were setting records in our business. I had never wanted to continue operating in such a small territory and the winter we had just passed through was below zero. Still, the focus was on what we loved about the assignment.

You break out of your cell, when you can live your life,

every part of your life, in the present with engaged joy and deep appreciation while eagerly reaching for something more.

"Cultivate the habit of being grateful for every good thing that comes to you, and to give thanks continuously. And because all things have contributed to your advancement, you should include all things in your gratitude."
Ralph Waldo Emerson

Strong in the Storm

Paul, operations manager for an equipment rental company in Longview, Washington, told us: "In October of 1981, my brother committed suicide. The following months there was a parade of visiting relatives from back east.

"During the summer of 1982, my cousin and grandmother visited. During their stay, a devastating story surfaced. My cousin told my wife and others in my family that I was an illegitimate child. My wife was inconsolable, with great difficulty and many tears; she told me the unbelievable story. By that time in my life, I had developed a thick skin and disregarded it as malicious gossip.

Unfortunately, my cousin and grandmother had already returned to Washington, and wouldn't return my calls. To my surprise, I was unable to reach any of my other relatives. Seemingly, overnight, my own family blackballed me. My parents had been divorced for many years and I had not spoken to my father in a long time. I decided the only way to resolve this issue was to ask my mother and put an end to this farce.

"I confronted her with the story being circulated and asked her if my father actually was my father. Her response was astounding. She said, 'No comment,' turned and walked away. I was heartbroken, and knew I was truly without a family.

"The following year, I hated, without remorse, compassion, or regard for anything or anyone. I was a negative, uncaring, bitter person who had given up on everything and everyone.

"At the time, I was working as a commercial fisherman in the Puget Sound. My skipper, Captain Jack, was always in a good mood. One night, as the boat thrashed about, I told my story to Jack. I explained my sudden expulsion from my family. I was so bitter and felt like I was worthless, with no sense of identity.

"Jack looked at me with that ever-happy glint in his eye and said, 'Paul, you're here now, and I love you. As for your family of origin, the strongest is he who stands most alone.'

"The lesson I learned from those turbulent years of searching for a safe harbor, is that my best friend must be in my heart."

The path to breaking free, to earning a lasting pardon, is learning to love yourself in spite of your family of origin, the faults and mis-deeds of your parents. Learning to see yourself as a unique creation, whole and complete, endowed by your creator with certain inalienable rights. Love your life for what it is, what it has been, and what it can be.

Those who have known the greatest sorrows, experienced the greatest hurts, can know the greatest joy and experience the greatest peace. Imagining, believing and accepting this truth may be the beginning for you as you resolve to pardon yourself and exit any cell, which may have been falsely holding you back.

"The more the marble wastes, the more the statue grows."

Michelangelo

David

The first time I saw Michelangelo's seventeen-foot-tall sculpture of David at the far end of the Galleria dell'Accademia museum in the heart of Florence, Italy, it was an awe-inspiring experience. Upon completion of his sculpture Angel of Arca di San Domenico Michelangelo said, "I saw the angel in the marble and carved until I set him free." The more marble you cut away that doesn't belong, the closer you come to creating the beautiful sculpture you desire. The same holds true for you and me. The more you rid yourself of the old, limiting thinking and beliefs that hold you back, the closer you come to being the person you desire to be. It does take effort. Michelangelo worked tirelessly for three long years to create David. He kept at it and set a new standard for renaissance art. So, even though it will take lengthy effort, keep chipping away at your limiting beliefs and delight your world with your new standard of excellence.

"Create the kind of self you will be happy to live with all your life."
Foster C. McClellan

The Persian Prince

Have you heard the story of the Persian prince who was born with a hunchback?

It was his destiny to one day be king. But, he was deformed to the point many in the kingdom could barely stand to think of the day when the deformed prince would assume the throne. The king loved the young prince very much; perhaps he loved him more because of his deformity. On his twelfth birthday, the king called the prince into the palace and asked what he wanted for his birthday. The King said he would give him anything within his royal kingdom he asked for. The prince replied, "I want a marble statue carved of me to be placed in the royal courtyard." When the king heard the request, he was so pained that the anguish showed on his face. The young prince said, "Oh Father, not bent over and crippled as I stand before you now, but rather I want the marble statue carved straight and tall."

The king commanded the royal sculptor to carve the prince's statue out of the finest white marble. The sculptor chiseled the shimmering stone into a figure that looked exactly as the adult prince would look if he had no deformity, straight and tall.

When the sculpture was finished, the king placed the beautiful effigy in the center of the palace garden. Then every single day the young prince stood before the statue and strained as he stared up into the eyes of his own likeness.

One day, a palace aid was heard to remark to another that it seemed the prince was standing straighter. This fired the prince's enthusiasm. He continued his daily ritual and worked even harder to bend his back straight as he stared at his white marble likeness.

The days passed quickly as they always do until the prince's 21st birthday. As he stood before the marble statue he had at first struggled to look up at, now, he was standing just as straight, erect, tall, and handsome as the statue.

Take a lesson from this ancient story of the Persian prince. Metaphorically carve a statue of yourself – envision how you want to be seen; draft a description of this ideal you. Hold this picture in your mind every day. Stand before the mental statue of who you wish to be. Then project yourself into this image. Like the Hunchback Persian Prince, one day you will experience the thrill of having your imagined reality match the perfected you which you envision.

Over the past decades, I have witnessed the closing of the gap between current reality and desired destiny in my life and in the lives of thousands in our programs. You can experience this closing of the gap. It starts by designing the life you wish for. Start today carving out a likeness of your perfect you. Mold the qualities you desire; courteous, brave, strong, and true. Sculpt the behaviors you wish to portray: promptness, organized, kept promises. Create the attitudes you want to reflect: enthusiasm, joy, confidence, humility. Stand before the image every day and soon people will be saying, "There's something about you that's different." And most important, you will be proud of the reflection you see each time you look in the mirror.

"Forgiveness does not change the past,
but it does enlarge the future."
Paul Boese

Singing for Your Supper

Dan, an electrician for a large timber company in south central Oregon, told us how he broke out of jail: "Seems like I've been singing since I was born. In high school, I was selected to All-State chorus three years in a row. I also received selection to the All-Northwest chorus in my senior year. Then I traveled to the University of Wyoming to apply for a music scholarship. I sang 'La Donna Mobile' for my piece. It was so well received I was awarded a full scholarship to sing opera.

"When I got back home, I was excited and couldn't wait to share my great success with my parents. I will never forget my father's words, 'I won't have one of my sons selling pantyhose for a living.' I felt total rejection. I was in shock and dismayed.

After a heated exchange, it was clear I must follow in the family business. Resentment welled up like a flood. I did all I could to distance myself from my parents. I did stay active in music. In 1982, I was given the lead in a production by the Casper, Wyoming Comic Opera Company. Monty Henrie, an extraordinary character, was the founder of the company. He had performed at the New York Met, so I asked Monty if he thought I could have made it to big time opera. He told me I could have gone as far as I wanted.

"That night, I reflected on the decision my father made for me five years earlier. My father was one of thirteen brothers and sisters from a poor farming family. He grew up hard and knew he could never help me with my music. I realized that my parents' decisions came from love and concern. I am happy to say my relationship with my parents is now very close."

You have nothing to prove. Feeling that you need to prove something or get even with them will keep you in jail forever. This is especially true if you try to prove that your parents were wrong, or have to prove what you could have done if you really tried, or they hadn't stopped you, or prove your teachers wrong when they said something degrading about you.

You will break free and advance to your greatness, your potential when you forgive and let go of past hurts and resentment. You must stop trying to justify your shortcomings by punishing your parents or tattling on your teachers. This is your life, so set your aim and hit your targets.

"A dream is your creative vision for your life in the future.
You must break out of your current comfort zone
and become comfortable with the unfamiliar and the unknown."
Dennis Waitley

Moving On

Christine, a department store manager, told us how she broke out of jail: "My parents have some great qualities. I am sure they loved their children, but I've spent most of my adult lives trying to figure out what went wrong. I have accepted that my dad was an alcoholic and my mom was depressed and addicted to denial. The rule was to put up a good front. We lived like gypsies, without roots in family or community.

"I had a profoundly retarded older sister. I remember her as a great wrestling partner. One day, when I was three and she was five, we left her at an institution and we never returned. I never knew why and we never talked about it.

"In my family it was my job to be adorable and slightly outrageous. I was the funny one. We were always 'the renters' in the neighborhoods we lived in. We didn't belong to anything. Every time we fixed up a cheesy rental house, we moved. Once I counted 43 moves! I went to eight different high schools; I spent more time out of school than in.

"Then I met a boy from a stable family who had a life insurance policy. Just barely eighteen years old, and pregnant, I marched down the aisle. Two months later, alone in a cheap little apartment, I lost the baby. No one ever knew and we never talked about it.

"I embraced a matronly, middle-class subdivision life. I looked older then than I do now, some 25 years later. At one point, I wrote a letter to my mother asking for some answers to the questions about my youth. She told me that they all had a good laugh about my letter. We never talked about it again.

"My first marriage ended in divorce. Actually, I married and divorced three abusive, alcoholic men. The more dysfunctional they were, the more I could focus on their problems and be the peacemaker, the fixer. After all, if I could fix them then maybe I could fix my broken childhood.

"My new life began at 40 when I moved to Portland. Single at last, I finally went to work on me. I found professional success and personal satisfaction. Then God sent me a real husband who loves me for me. Together we made my first happy home.

"When I joined the Leadership Development Lab I dug deeper. I saw that my old ways wouldn't work. My sarcastic, outrageous remarks are not necessary. I had never successfully confronted a problem my whole life. Instead, I found ways to cope, bury my anger, and be debilitated by insecurity. I am beginning to understand the concepts of empowerment; of open, non-combative confrontation. I am opening up and emptying out my black bag of pain, anger, grudges and sorrow.

"Am I out of my comfort zone? You bet! But, in retrospect, it never was comfortable in there. Healing feels much better."

Your pardon requires a willingness and ability to break with some traditions in your family of origin. You must leave behind some of your deeply inherited beliefs about yourself and others.

We all have a limiting *circum*-stance. We stand in a circle that was drawn by our past. It only determines our future if we submit, give in, resign to this inherited pattern. This is the natural, easy thing to do. It is unnatural to leave your past, your tribe behind but the rewards are worth it. To do this, you must create a new story, you must design a new you.

"Life is too short to hold a grudge, also too long."
Robert Brault

Blind Love

Nancy, department manager at a major retailer, told us how she broke out of jail: "On October 4, 1990 I received a phone call from my sister in Maryland telling me my mother had died. This was a tremendous shock because it was so unexpected. My mother and I had always been especially close. She had been one of my best friends. I felt a part of me died with that phone call. Another reason my mother's death was especially traumatic was the circumstances surrounding it. My mother was blind and falling was one of her greatest fears. She died because of a fall down a flight of stairs. The reason she fell was that my father, an alcoholic, left the door at the top of the stairs wide open. Then he didn't call for medical help. My mother died several hours later because of head injuries.

"I experienced many conflicting emotions. I had not been close to my father for several years and now I wasn't sure how I would feel when I saw him. I realized he would be hurting terribly. I could either help him through this terrible time or add to his suffering. I chose to show him my love and give him my support because I knew he would need it.

"For nearly two years both of us worked on our relationship and stayed in close touch. It is a time I cherish and will always remember. My dad died suddenly, less than two years after my mother's death, and I was saddened by it. I am thankful for the action I took and the relationship that developed as a result.

"The lesson I learned from my experience is that it's important for me to concentrate on the positive and stay in relationship. When I take the first steps and the extra steps required to repair and renew broken relationships, good things can come out of bad times."

One of the things that can hold you back, keep you in jail is having an attachment to your story of how you have been hurt and victimized. When you hold a grudge, your identity, your self-image, becomes attached. You have to want the freedom of the pardon more than you want to remain the author and owner of your limiting, imprisoning story.

Forgiveness is not about letting the other person off the hook for their behavior. Forgiveness doesn't say, "What you did was OK or acceptable." Forgiveness is about letting yourself off the emotional hook. It is releasing the negative hold resentment has on you.

The value of forgiveness is for you, not the other person. For example, let's say your parents did something to you years ago, and you have not been able to forgive them. Let's say they died. How can you forgive them? Isn't it too late? Yes, it is too late to tell them you forgive them. They have died. It is not too late to send forgiveness to them, thereby releasing the grief, pain, or anxiety that holding onto this lack of forgiveness causes you.

Why is it so hard to forgive? Do we really need to hold on to unforgiveness about anything anyone has ever done or said to us? When we believe someone needs our forgiveness, we assume they did something to cause us pain.

Who do you need to forgive and why? Remember, forgiveness is not about the other person. It is about who you are, who you are becoming and the quality of your life – and yours alone.

It is amazing what good things can come about when you forgive and let go of the past. Energy that was misdirected all of a sudden turns into a force for the betterment of all – especially you. It is so easy to hang on to past hurts, but no one wins. It may seem tough to let go, but the winner as you release will be you. So, as a winning way of thinking, look back and see if there is anyone, or any situation, that still burns a hole in you, and then make up your mind right now that all of that is gone. You will earn your pardon and you will be free to experience a larger life than you've ever known before.

All of us have someone in our life who has messed up something. Each of us, to some degree, are holding onto that past. Do you see that when you are holding on to disappointment or anger you could be held back?

The prescription for resolution is this; if there is something to say, say it. Muster as much resolution as you can, take appropriate action, and move on. If you hold onto negative feelings and expectations, you will unconsciously and perhaps consciously, create more of the same. You need to be prepared for and expect their best if you hope to see improvement.

Many people blame the present on the past at the expense of the life and love available now. Your past does not bind you, unless you choose to carry it with you like a backpack. Too many individuals, families, nations, punish themselves by digging up harmful memories repeatedly. Ben Cohen and Shoshana Hadad had a rude awakening when the State of Israel told them their marriage was not legal because Shoshana's noble ancestor married a peasant – in 580 B.C. That is a 2,500 year punishment!

Have you been punishing yourself or someone else for something that happened a long time ago? Any payoff you perceive for holding a grudge is an illusion; there is no value, only a weighty price. In the throes of anger or rage, all kinds of chemicals surge into our body that exact a heavy toll on our health and vitality.

True forgiveness is "selective forgetting." Your pain comes not from what happened to you in the past, but from holding onto painful memories. It is within your power to release the thoughts that trouble you. You can change thoughts that hurt by replacing them with thoughts that help.

Just keep on letting go. We must remember that forgiveness is more of a gift to ourselves than to the person we are forgiving.

"Forgiveness is the attribute of the strong."
Mahatma Gandhi

Shoe Shopping

Jayne Ann, the executive secretary for a major Oregon general contractor, told us: "On April 3, 1984, my 17-year marriage ended. My daughters were 15 and 16-years-old. In December of that same year about six months later, my oldest daughter decided to live with her dad. She has not spent a night with me since. Through the course of the past 14 years, all we've done is fight and argue. She got to the point of not even recognizing my birthday, Christmas, or even Mother's Day.

"After the first session of the LDL, my daughter and our painful relationship came forcibly to mind many times. When the 15 Leadership Principles were discussed and memorized: see the other person's point of view, listen, and praise; don't argue; say yes, yes, yes, and so on, I began to believe there was hope for us - we could talk. Then came the "Pearl" assignment, and we were challenged to improve our relationship with someone either at work or in our personal lives. Instantly I knew who my "Pearl" would be. The next morning I called my daughter and said, 'Let's meet in Vegas.' Without hesitation, she said, 'Yes, why don't you make the reservations?' I did and we met last weekend. Never once did we say a crossword. Never once did anything ugly happen. What we found out was that we hold a lot in common, many of the same tastes (all great, of course). I ordered a Reuben sandwich for lunch and she said, 'Mom, I didn't know you liked Reubens.' My normal reaction would have been, 'There are lots of things you don't know about me because you weren't around.' Because of the 15 Leadership

Principles I committed to applying, I replied, 'Yes, I do, would you like to split one?'

"I discovered my daughter has grown into a wonderful responsible woman and deserves to be treated as a mature lady, not as a teenager. I finally understood the pain she went through was on a different level than the hurt I experienced. I realized I need to forget the past, live now, and look forward to a meaningful relationship with her in the years that lay ahead.

"I gained respect for my daughter, and started to develop the relationship I have always wanted. I gained the feeling that she is beginning to respect me, and, to boot, we can party together!"

If you want a 'Get Out of Jail Free Card,' I challenge you to employ the leadership principle "Be an Active Listener" when dealing with difficult people, hold your tongue and listen. Remember the feelings of others; be careful not to be resentful, or disrespectful of their feelings and experience.

The weak hold grudges, try to get even, harbor resentment. Exercising forgiveness of those who knowingly or unknowingly hurt you frees you from the past. You lighten your load. There is a new bounce in your step, a greater erectness in your gait; you step forward to meet a greater fate.

Practice this affirmation, "I release the past. I break free to live a life of liberty."

If you have been carrying a grudge bag, cut out the bottom of the bag and let the grudges fall through. How do we cut the bottom out of the grudge bag? Here is an idea. Sit down and make a list of all the people you think hurt you, offended you, slandered you, cheated you, broke their promises, or were not honest in other ways with you. As you make your list, be completely honest with yourself. List everyone, yes - everyone. Write out, "I forgive ______.for ______. I forgive myself for ______." Write it. Then rewrite it. Repeat it over and over until you finally mean it and your feeling of forgiveness is complete. This can be painful because it requires bringing to the surface old, painful experiences you may tried to stuff. If you truly forgive, there will be no more pain. If there is pain, you have not completely forgiven and you could be suffering from low-grade anger that will drain your energy.

"Life is ten percent what happens to you and ninety percent how you respond to it."
Lou Holtz

Over the past 30 years, my experience in working with over 4,800 upper, middle, and frontline managers in the Leadership Development Lab has taught me that none of us live fairy tale lives. Though the fairy tale of "Cinderella" may be charming, the reality is none of us live free of hurt, betrayal, disappointment, and setback. The difference in those whose lives are meaningful, rich, inspirational examples for others isn't the amount of difficulty they encounter; it is their ability to handle that difficulty, to exercise resilience, they bounce back, and move on with a life that is full of purpose and meaning. My challenge to you is to examine any resentment you may be holding onto, any past pain that may be diminishing the quality of your life. Decide today to put it behind you. You will escape the prison of your past and live a life filled with direction, meaning, and purpose.

Before we leave this chapter, give yourself the gift of a powerful, positive *life sentence.*

Start by looking back over your day. What is one thing you did or said today that you are proud of?

Then read this list of positive qualities and circle the ones you 'lived-out' today.

Adaptable
Ambitious
Attentive
Bright
Committed
Considerate
Convincing
Courageous
Creative
Decisive
Determined
Dynamic
Enthusiastic
Generous
Honest
Humble
Innovative
Insightful
Open-minded
Optimistic
Persistent
Persuasive
Precise
Productive
Proficient
Resourceful
Responsible
Spontaneous
Supportive
Tenacious
Thorough
Thoughtful

Hold that picture in mind. What quality did you draw on? Now you are ready.

Start by stating aloud your own name, followed by a description of how you acted today. It might sound like this: *"____Larry____,you are precise. The way you wrote that client email today shows how precise you can be. As you continue to exercise clarity in your communication, you will reach your goals quickly."*

Please don't turn the page until you have given yourself an empowering *life sentence*.

Preparation for Tomorrow

Now, highlight one of the desirable qualities listed that you want to demonstrate more of tomorrow.

Take the time to envision how you look acting that way. Imagine someone praising you for demonstrating this positive quality.

Chapter Four

"What lies behind us and what lies before us are tiny matters compared to what lies within us."
Henry David Thoreau

LIVING A LIBERATED LIFE

Early Start

Shelley, supervisor for a restaurant chain in Yakima, Washington, told us: "About fifteen years ago, I jumped out of bed around 3:30 in the morning. This was about two-and-a-half hours earlier than normal. I started getting ready for work a little faster than usual.

"I went through my usual routine – showered, dressed quietly – I didn't want to disturb my husband who was still sound asleep. I put my hair up, dabbed on a little makeup, and walked as quietly as possible out the front door. The previous night I backed into the driveway because I knew it would be dark the next morning when I was leaving at a little past 4:00 a.m. When I got into my car, I continued my routine – started the engine, buckled up, put the car in reverse, and hit the gas. I heard a loud bang as I backed INTO our garage door! The garage door was still standing, so I drove on to work. When I walked into my office, the phone was ringing. It was my husband. In spite of all my preparation and efforts not to disturb him, he was wide-awake!

"The lesson I learned from this experience is that I am a creature of habit. Much of what I do is completely automatic."

"Yes" Shelley is a creature of habit and so are you. I will say with great certainty most of your habits are very good. To live a liberated life you must change a few, not all, of your habits.

I have asked thousands, in audiences to give me an example of a habit. I hear "brushing your teeth" and "smoking." These are examples of behavior habits. Shelly's wonderful story of backing into the garage door is an example of a behavior habit.

We also have attitude habits, feelings we automatically experience when conditions change, the feeling of joy or letdown, exhilaration or deflation, expectations or dread. Feelings you automatically assume without thinking are attitude habits. You know people who seem to be positive regardless of the circumstance and others who are negative about any change. We even created names for them. We call them an optimist or a pessimist.

The third kind of habits are self-image habits. Self-image is the way you see yourself. You weren't born with a self-image. You learned the image you have of yourself. Do you think you see yourself accurately? Do you tend to sell yourself short or sell yourself long? Your self-image, the picture you hold of yourself regulates your initiative, persistence, creativity, your interactions with others, and the risks you are willing to take. Your self-image habits, just as the way you brush your teeth habits, can be changed. You can learn to see yourself differently. Ultimately, your self-image determines what you do, your actions, and how you feel, your attitudes. For you to live a liberated life, truly free of the limiting cells of the past, you must change some of your behaviors, attitudes, and self-image habits.

"Destiny is no matter of chance.
It is a matter of choice. It is not a thing to be waited for,
it is a thing to be achieved."
William Jennings Bryan

I'm In the Army Now

After being accepted into The W. Bingham Company's sales training program, my first job was working as an order picker on the 12th floor of the warehouse. I needed to become thoroughly familiar with our processes, customers, and merchandise. After less than nine months, I was promoted to a customer account service position. I processed return goods credits for retail hardware store accounts of 19 of our 93 salesmen. After six months, I settled into the job. In the summer of 1959, before my 19th birthday, the sales representative for Euclid, Ohio asked me to cover his territory while he took a vacation. After two-weeks of "carrying the catalog," I was eager to be assigned my own territory. But, it was apparent that I would be sitting at the desk for the next four years or longer. I was simply too young to be assigned a territory.

Frank, who was on the desk next to me, had been in the office for almost three years, when he was assigned a territory. A year-and-a-half later, he was drafted. When discharged from the army he was put back on a desk again! He expected to be on the desk for two or three years before being assigned a new sales territory.

I made what I thought was a good strategic decision. I would get my required military service behind me. If I joined any one of the services, it would be a 4-year commitment. My long-term objective was to be a professional salesperson. After work and on Saturdays, I visited recruiting officers at each of the military branches. I knew there were no salespeople in the service, but there were certainly purchasing officers. I wanted to be in purchasing while I was in the service so I could see things from the other side of the desk. Each time I told a recruiter what I wanted to do while I was in the service; they laughed at me and told me all purchasing was done at the Pentagon. Then they offered me electronic school. I laughed at them and decided to volunteer for the draft and keep my required service down to two years. In a matter of days, I received my notice. Frank's parting advice – "Never volunteer for anything."

My dream of being a purchasing agent hadn't left me. After basic training at Fort Lewis, Missouri, I was shipped off to Fort Eustis, Virginia. Everyone was given their orders and we were all trying to figure out what our Military Occupational Specialty (MOS) orders meant. I was devastated when I found out my number meant "stevedore." For the next two years, I'd be loading and unloading ships in the US Army Transportation Corp. I was disappointed. After all the testing and screening, was that the best use of my skills? I decided to volunteer for any job that came my way. Over the next few months, I was a parts man, a mechanic, a carpenter, the commanding officers' chauffer, and chaplain's assistant.

I was determined to earn as many college credits as possible while in the Army. When I visited the Fort Story Post Education office, I learned they had a basic math class starting in a few weeks. I didn't need basic math. I knew the Army was obligated to arrange for transportation to night school. I had just enrolled at William and Mary when my unit was ordered to Goose Bay, Labrador. I struggled with the transfer, even had a special audience with my Commanding Officer. I told him I had enrolled in classes in Norfolk, Virginia. He wasn't very sympathetic. He said, "When we get to Goose Bay, you can start classes there." When our unit arrived in Labrador, I did enroll. Then only a few weeks later I was transferred to a temporary 90-day assignment in Sondrestrom, Greenland. While there, I was honored as "Soldier of the Month."

Soon, I was back in Goose Bay. Suffice it to say, I never did attend night school there. Over the months, I became good friends with Virgil Casto, who was a clerk at our Company

Headquarters. He told me my entry test scores were the highest in the unit. I decided when we got back to Fort Story, I was going to do everything I could to get a new, permanent MOS.

Within twenty-four hours of arriving back at the post, I went to our Company Headquarters and asked about job opportunities. I also went to the Education Office to see Dennis Denahae. They told me he transferred and was in a purchasing role for the Fort. When I located him, I said, "I thought you would be discharged by now." He told me he only had a few more days to go. There was a little panic on the base because they couldn't find anyone with an outgoing personality who could communicate competently to take his place. On Dennis' recommendation, I went straight to the Fort Headquarters to see the Base Commanding Officer. We had a quick meeting and I went back to my company area. As it turned out, a Sergeant had spotted me at company headquarters and reported me to my Commanding Officer. I was out of my area without permission, technically AWOL (Absent Without Official Leave). After a forceful, profanity punctuated reprimand behind closed doors; I was transferred to Base Headquarters Company on Thanksgiving Day. I was thankful to be the new Ordering Officer for Fort Story, Virginia! For the rest of my time in the service, each day the Purser gave me orders and the cash required to buy the supplies needed for the Fort. I wore my Class A uniform and drove a military vehicle into Norfolk to purchase the supplies the Fort needed. I went to lunch with company owners, were acquainted with the managers of supply houses, and grew in many ways over the next 18 months.

Another part of your program for living a liberated life is to set specific goals. Set stretching, tangible, do, be, have goals in all six areas of your life: social, mental, physical, spiritual, financial, and family. Remember what Robert Browning said,

"Ah, but a man's reach should exceed his grasp, or what's a heaven for?" Avoid the defeating "obtainable" or "attainable" adjective as you set your goals. Set high goals. Goals that will cause you to stretch. James Collins and Jerry Porras called them "big, hairy, audacious goals." Develop the best plan you can and most importantly – go into action. Often on the road to achieving your goals you will find new pathways, new avenues and help you couldn't have imagined. You must go into action!

"Opportunity is often difficult to recognize;
we usually expect it to beckon us with beepers and billboards."
William A. Ward

Batman's Buckle

Tona, a senior field consultant for Subway Development Corporation, told us: "It was 1992, and I was a waitress at the Village Inn Restaurant in Salem while attending Western Oregon State College. It was 11:30 p.m. - only thirty minutes until closing. It had been a long day and we were short-handed. I hadn't even had a dinner break. I was tired, hungry, and just wanted to go home. Suddenly, customers started pouring through the door. Within minutes, almost every table was full, and the restaurant seated over a hundred people!

"There was only one other waitress and myself. It was a nightmare. It is literally, physically impossible to wait on that many customers at once. We were frantic, brewing coffee, running back and forth from the kitchen. It must have taken 45 minutes before I finally got to a table in back where a party of 7 or 8 people was seated. One customer looked so familiar to me; I kept asking myself, 'Where do I know him from?' However, I was too busy to sort it out. I thought, he has probably eaten here before. I went around the table taking orders, when I finally got to this man. Instead of giving his order, he said, 'Do you like my belt buckle? I won it today.'

"'Who is this guy?' I thought. Food is getting cold on the counter, people are calling, 'Miss, Miss, more coffee', and he's making small talk. 'That's really nice' I said, 'But, as you can see, I am very busy. If you are not going to order, you'll have to wait until I have time, and that's definitely going to be a while.' Irritation definitely came out in my tone of voice. 'Well, you make a chef salad, don't you? I'll order that.'

"Later, as all the customers finally started leaving, this gentleman's party left. Every customer in the restaurant stared at them as they walked by the front windows. 'There he goes,' one customer said, 'Batman!'

"'That's who that guy looks like!' I said, 'Michael Keaton.' All the customers started laughing at me. 'That is Michael Keaton,' someone said, and they handed me a program from a Cutting Horse Rodeo held that day in Salem, which featured several major celebrities, including Michael Keaton."

"The lesson I learned from this experience is the importance of treating everyone like they are a celebrity, so I can always be proud of my performance."

A part of your program for living a liberated life is treating every customer, every co-worker, everyone you encounter as though they are the celebrity you most admire. As you make a habit of treating everyone with patience and kindness, as you would a celebrity, you will admire yourself even more. This personal pride will propel you forward.

"Courage is not the absence of fear; it is control of fear, mastery of fear."
Mark Twain

Life Saver

Doug, scaffold manager, Ivy Hi-Lift, Portland, Oregon told us: "A few years ago I went through our hedge to the adjoining church playground next door. I was shocked to find my little nephew, Craig, lying unconscious with a serious head wound. He had fallen from the playground slide. I raced to the house and told my wife to call 911. My brother and I ran back to administer first aid. It was automatic. I did what I had been taught to do in our company CPR classes. Thankfully, he recovered with only a slight hearing loss in one ear.

"Several months later, my brother's family was at our house when I heard my wife scream from the backyard. I raced back there to find my other nephew, Chad, had fallen in our shallow pond. He had no pulse and was not breathing. My wife called 911 and I started CPR. I breathed into his lungs, but the air would not exit. I pushed down on his stomach trying to help him. I repeated the procedure until he finally expelled large quantities of food and water. Then he started to breathe on his own. To my amazement, the medic who arrived was the same person who responded months earlier with Craig.

"About a year later, I heard another scream from my wife. This time, it was our 18-month-old son. He had somehow managed to climb into the back of my truck, pull the nozzle out of the spare gas can and inhale it as if it was a big straw. The fumes collapsed his esophagus. His face and hands were blue. Every muscle in his body spasmed. He was going to die. I pried his mouth open so I could clear his airway and he began to breathe again.

"I was sitting on the couch crying my heart out and mumbling about what I had done wrong. The same ambulance driver grabbed me and said, 'What you've done is save three precious little boys lives in two years, so lighten up on yourself."

Living a liberated life means, you are as prepared as possible for the unexpected emergencies that come your way. Everyone is afraid. You're afraid. I'm afraid. Everyone you meet is afraid in some way, often in many ways. The brave person is the person who acts in spite of their fear, who faces the fear, feels the fear, and moves forward anyway.

"Cowards die many times before their deaths,
the valiant never taste of death but once."
William Shakespeare

Stormy Waters

Steve, foreman for Cascade Acoustics, told us, "It was a stormy day in 1968 in Kodiak, Alaska on the U.S. Coast Guard Cutter Yacona #268. We received a distress call. A fishing vessel needed assistance because their engines were not operational, and the vessel had taken on a lot of water. The weather conditions were at 'whole gale', winds blowing at between 80 to 100-miles per hour, the sea in 30 to 40-foot swells.

"Our ship was under way immediately, heading out to help the fishing vessel. The storm was amazingly strong. As the ship thrust forward, plunging into and through the waves, most of the crew was seasick.

"When we arrived at the fishing vessel the waves were tremendous; they were tossing the ship around like a little cork. We knew that someone had to swim over to the fishing vessel to either take the crew off or start the engines. The Coast Guard crewmember assigned to emergency rescues was very seasick, and I was the next in line. I wastrained for this, but had never used the skill in a real life situation. I didn't know if I could do it, but I knew I must because there were people's lives at stake. We threw a rope over to the fishing vessel. I put on my dry suit and got the equipment I thought I would need. I hooked my safety harness onto the lifeline and jumped into the raging sea. I didn't realize how huge the waves were until I got into the sea, they were gigantic. I swam over, got on board, and made sure the crew was okay. I talked to the captain to scope out the situation and then I headed to the engine compartment to see if I could fix it. I tested the fuel line that went to the fuel pump. It was getting fuel, so that was not the problem. I reconnected the fuel line, took off the high-pressure side, turned over the engine and there was nothing. I found the problem was the fuel pump. As it turned out, their engine was the same engine we used for our generators. I radioed back to the ship to send me a new fuel pump. I installed it and started the engine. The captain started the bilge pump and turned the fishing vessel back into the huge waves. I stayed aboard to ride out the storm in case something else went wrong. When we got back to Kodiak, they awarded me the Lifesaving medal.

"The lesson I learned from this experience is when the sea is raging, if I am prepared through training, I can handle almost anything."

This too is part of your program for liberated living. Prepare yourself for all of the opportunities that might come your way. Be aware of your fears but let your heart be your guide. Prepare yourself with specialized training so you will act with courage. Take the plunge and you will receive the recognition and rewards you deserve.

"The earlier you admit to your mistakes,
the more time you would have to learn and grow from them."
Edmond Mbiaka

Sad Saab Story

John, weekend manager for Georgie's Ceramics, told us: "It was 1980, I had just gotten married, and my new brother-in-law, David, asked me if I would bring to readiness one of my restorable classic Saab's for him. I had been restoring classic Saab's as a hobby for years and had rebuilt eleven vehicles from the ground up. I told him I would be glad to help, and we began the rebuilding of my personal favorite, an eight-year-old 1972 Saab wagon. Fortunately, for us it was a very clean car to start with. I rebuilt the engine and transaxle, re-did the brakes, clutch, and the interior, and gave it a beautiful new paint job. It was looking good inside and out! I thought I had prepared and checked everything. I looked it over one last time for any errors or mistakes. It looked perfect, better than when it rolled off the production line in Sweden. He was excited; I gave him the keys, and sent him on his way.

"A couple of hours later, he returned and said, 'Everything was running great except that it seemed a little hard to shift. There seemed to be a howling noise coming from the engine compartment." As he said this, I glanced toward the garage and saw two unopened bottles of transaxle oil sitting on my workbench. My heart sank to my stomach. I accepted responsibility and nervously pointed out my error."

An important part of your program for liberated living – "When you blow it, show it." Admit your faults, errors, and mistakes. Always be quick to admit your mistakes – it saves a lot of time. Sometimes, no matter how hard you try, things will go wrong. When mistakes happen and it is your responsibility, admit it. Don't make excuses, accept responsibility. Then ask the question "What part did I play in this?" Whether it is your fault or not, the facts are the same, face forward, and move on. By accepting responsibility, you will be able to learn from all your experiences, especially your mistakes. Your willingness to admit your mistakes and accept responsibility will set you apart as a respected leader and build your confidence at the core.

Part of your program for liberated living is to be a problem-solver, not a speck-spotter. Find out what the real problem is and fix it instead of jumping to hasty conclusions.

"A rock pile ceases to be a rock pile
the moment a single person
contemplates it bearing within them the image of a cathedral."
Antoine de Saint-Expupéry

Going Forward

Remember you are an "imagineer." Everything in your world was first a thought before it became a thing. We all know this. We forget how powerful it is to use this creative faculty of mind.

Your past is not prologue. Never has been, never will be. Your past does not determine your future. Regardless of your past, the power lies within you to live a liberated life. None of us uses our imagination to its full potential. Create a beautiful picture, like a movie on the screen of your mind, of the life you would love to live. Then, play this movie of your life every night before you go to sleep. You will be free of your past to live a liberated life.

"We change the world not by what we say or do,
but as a consequence of what we have become."
Dr. David R. Hawkins

Before you close the covers of LIFE SENTENCES for the last time – craft the movie you want to star in.

The kind of friend you are eager to be?

The kind of spouse you desire to be?

The kind of parent you wish to be?

The kind of employee you need to be?

The kind of boss you aspire to be?

Answer each question as something you see on the movie screen of your mind. Make your movie in 3D, IMAX, HD, THX, virtual reality. Describe each scene with as many of the five senses as you can imagine.

"Though no one can go back and make a brand new start, anyone can start from now and make a brand new ending."

Carl Bard

ABOUT THE AUTHOR

Larry W. Dennis, Sr. is the energetic founder of **Turbo Leadership Systems**™. Larry has been helping businesses in the US and Canada improve their profits and performance for over thirty years.

Larry is a life-long learner who designs and implements customized leadership development programs for teams of progressive companies, leading to the improved performance and profits.

Larry is also the inventor of the patented media training system, *Psycho-Actualized Learning (PAL).* He is a dedicated father, and grandfather of seven who has been profiled in *Secrets of Raising Teenagers Successfully.* He is listed in Who's Who of the World, a member of the International Platform Association, serves on his church board, the Providence Newberg Health Foundation, and the Cascade Policy Institute board.

TURBO
LEADERSHIP SYSTEMS®

"Empowering your team
to ensure continuous improvement."

For more information about Larry W. Dennis, Sr and
Turbo Leadership Systems™

www.turbols.com
larry@turbols.com
cell 503-329-4519

To order books, please visit
www.turbols.com/turbo_books.html